ECSTASY

ECSTASY:
Finding Joy
in Living

by Lester Sumrall

Thomas Nelson Publishers
Nashville

Old Testament Scripture quotations are from the *King James
Bible*. New Testament Scripture quotations are from the *New
King James Bible, New Testament*, © 1979 by Thomas Nelson
Publishers, Inc. Used by permission.

Second Printing

Library of Congress Cataloging in Publication Data

Sumrall, Lester Frank, 1913-
  Ecstasy : finding joy in living.

  1. Ecstasy. I. Title.
BV5091.E3S9   1980   248.4   80-284
ISBN 0-8407-5717-4

Contents

Preface

The writing of this book began on a Sunday evening as I flew from Chicago to Algeria. As we crossed the Atlantic on a 747 jetliner, I spent most of the night in meditation and prayer, reaching out to God through my spirit. I longed to know what God wanted me to do with my ministry. What mission did He have for me? What message did He want me to give the thousands of people who watch my broadcasts?

The word *ecstasy* kept coming to my mind. It seemed to ripple through my spirit like a gentle melody: *ecstasy* . . . *ecstasy* . . . *ecstasy*. My mind fastened upon this word and I wondered, *How can I bring happiness, joy, and ecstasy to the hearts of my listeners?*

By Monday noon I had checked through customs and had found a hotel room in Algiers, the capital city of Algeria. The weather was very hot and humid, and the air conditioning was not working.

I returned to my room and tried to lie down and rest. But I was wide awake. My mind was spinning with ideas about the happiness God can bring to a person's life. I spent most of the night writing on this topic of ecstasy. It was fantastic. The presence of God was very near.

On Tuesday I visited several historic sites in Algiers and began recording my observations about the country's spiritual climate (which was the purpose of my visit). I saw Catholic churches that had been converted to Islamic mosques. Islamic religious officials lived in lavish homes and walked the halls of government. I saw no churches and no Christian missionary work.

I had every reason to feel depressed, yet when I returned to my room I found I was full of energy and excitement. I spent several more hours writing about the ecstasy of the Christian life.

On Wednesday morning I finished my fact-finding tour of Algeria and boarded a plane for Switzerland. Again that night I could not sleep. My heart seemed full of the message of Christian happiness, and I spent most of the night pouring out more chapters of the book.

I spent another night in Zurich. At last I dozed off for a couple of hours. But in the wee hours of the morning I was at the desk again, revising these studies on ecstasy. I felt an urgent need to finish the task. As the hours passed, I became more and more excited about the book. I realized that God wanted me to present the gospel in a forceful, positive way. He wanted me to share the truth of God-given happiness with this generation—speaking boldly instead of defensively, for the truth needs no defense. His message of faith and power sets the human spirit free.

That was the message He had given me, and it is the message I share with you here: "Therefore if the Son makes you free, you shall be free indeed" (John 8:36).

1

What Is Ecstasy?

Feasting on the riches of His grace,
Resting 'neath His shelt'ring wing,
Always looking on His smiling face—
That is why I shout and sing.
                          —Luther B. Bridges*

The psalmist knew the secret of happy living. He turned his face toward God and said, "Thou wilt shew me the path of life: in thy presence is fulness of joy; at thy right hand there are pleasures for evermore" (Ps. 16:11). If you live in the presence of God, you will know the fullness of life—the *ecstasy* of life—just as the psalmist did.

Our world has many misguided notions about ecstasy. Cheap paperback novels paint an enticing picture of adultery, prostitution, and sexual perversion that is supposed to give the reader a taste of "ecstasy." Sports commentators tell us that athletes enjoy the "ecstasy" of winning. Gamblers say that when a long shot pays off, they feel a sense of "ecstasy." But these temporary thrills are not real ecstasy.

Ecstasy: Finding Joy in Living

Webster tells us that ecstasy is "an overflowing of joy," "a state of rapture," or an experience of "intense delight." I think these are good definitions, but they only describe the characteristics of ecstasy. They do not describe the source of ecstasy.

God created us to know intense delight every day of our lives. But few people find much delight in living. Most Americans clamor for physical, sensual pleasure because they do not have the close relationship with God that would give them true happiness. They are hungering for something beyond the physical senses of the body, and they will not be happy until they find it.

A young couple gets married and settles down to a comfortable life in the suburbs. They both find rewarding, well-paying jobs. They make friends with neighbors and fellow employees. As the years go by, they bear children and experience all the joys and sorrows of being parents. They have good health, a good home, and good prospects for the future.

But then they get a divorce. Their friends ask them why. They give a long list of reasons and sum it up by saying, "We just didn't enjoy it anymore." I've seen this tragedy so many times that tears well up when I think about it.

Divorce is a common example of our nation's restless search for pleasure. Men and women keep looking for enjoyment, but they never find it.

Acts 8:8 tells us that when Philip went to preach the gospel in Samaria, "there was great joy in that city." Acts 8:39 says that when the Ethiopian eunuch received Christ, "he went on his way rejoicing." Christ always brings joy. He makes your spirit sing and your heart laugh. People can even tell by the way you walk that you feel happy in the Lord.

No wonder Satan tries to imitate the joys of the Christian life! No wonder he tries to lure people into a false sense of happiness! He says, "Follow your desires and you will be happy." He knows he is a liar, but most of the world doesn't. Most people realize too late that "there is a way which seemeth right unto a man, but the end thereof are the ways of death" (Prov. 14:12).

Joni Eareckson almost learned too late. Joni is a beautiful young woman who was paralyzed by a swimming accident in 1967. Before her accident, Joni was involved in a love affair with a young man. They gave free rein to their passions and indulged in physical love, even though they weren't married. Joni's accident ended their affair. It forced her to think about what she was doing with her life. She writes:

> Alone with God, I recalled how I'd withdrawn from reality and turned my back on Him so often. . . . The Holy Spirit began to convict, then teach me. With each succeeding week, spiritual truth became more real, and I began to see life from God's perspective. . . . With God's help and forgiveness, I repented and put all that behind me. I prayed for His direction and the mental will power to think His thoughts and not wallow in self-pity and lustful memories and fantasies.[1]

Jesus Christ enables us to do that. He enables us to turn our backs on the false joys of the world and plunge into the true joy of fellowship with our heavenly Father.

A man named Nicodemus marvelled at what Jesus was able to do. He said with a wistful sigh, "no one can do these signs that You do unless God is with him" (John 3:2). Nicodemus longed for a relationship with his heavenly Father that was as complete and trusting as the relationship Jesus had with him. So Jesus told Nicodemus, "Most assuredly, I say to you, unless one is born again, he cannot see the kingdom of God" (John 3:3). Only when a person is born into God's spiritual family can he know the ecstasy of a fulfilled life.

On the day of Pentecost, some people sneered at the behavior of Jesus' followers, saying they were "full of new wine" (Acts 2:13). The Christians were giddy from their experience with God's Holy Spirit; they were beside themselves with happiness. Perhaps you have not seen this kind of ecstatic joy in your church, but in the early church it was a distinctive mark of the Christians. It still is.

The Qualities of Ecstasy

In another chapter we will consider how Christ brings ecstasy to a person's life. But first let us consider the qualities of ecstasy. Webster attempted to describe this, and it is foremost in many people's minds today. How does true happiness feel? How does it affect our lives? What does ecstasy mean for our way of life?

Contentment

Ecstasy is the contentment of the total person. If your spirit is not happy, your body cannot be happy. For example, if you are dancing in a discotheque and your conscience says you should not be there, you cannot be happy—even if you pretend to be! Dr. Clyde M. Narramore, a noted Christian counselor, says this kind of double life gradually destroys every aspect of a person's well-being:

> Psychologists and psychiatrists know that a person cannot develop as he should if he harbors the feeling that he is guilty and sinful. It restricts and distorts his growth both emotionally and mentally. Since this is true, a sense of guilt is not a matter to be taken lightly.[2]

When Christ comes into a person's life, He takes away all sin and its guilt. He sets a person free from that burden. He allows that person to live a happy, victorious life in the light of God's grace. Solving exterior problems (such as the lack of money or the lack of fine clothes) will not bring happiness. But solving the interior problem of guilt—this brings happiness.

Think of it this way: You can whitewash a barn or you can wash it white. If you whitewash an old gray barn, the paint will soak in and you will see gray patches again. But if you wash a barn that's already painted white, you allow its true nature to shine through. That's how it is with your life. You can't whitewash unhappiness and expect it to go away. But if Christ—the Source of happiness—lives within you, His joy will shine through everything that may trouble you from the outside.

If you are doing what is right for both body and soul, your entire being is functioning harmoniously. That is ecstasy! This God-given experience unites and directs the complex human personality. When your spirit, your soul (mind, emotions, and will), and your five senses work in unison, you live in the mainstream of this ecstasy.

Ecstasy: Finding Joy in Living

Security

Psalm 23 was written in a state of ecstasy. Consider what the psalmist said: "The Lord is my shepherd; I shall not want" (v. 1). Those words express a deep sense of security. How can a person be happy without being secure?

At the end of World War II, the U.S. Army set up several field hospitals to care for refugee children in the occupied countries of Europe. These children did not know where their parents were, or even if they were still alive. Doctors noticed that the children were restless at night; they couldn't sleep, even after eating a hearty meal.

Finally, one of the doctors had an idea. The nurses would give every child a piece of bread at bedtime, but they would tell the children not to eat it. If the children were still hungry they could ask for more to eat, but the piece of bread was just there to be held.

It worked! The children began falling asleep at night. They knew they held their breakfast in their hands, and that was enough to reassure them. That's what security can do.

The psalmist told of living beside the "still waters" (Ps. 23:2). Surely there were difficult times in his life, but they did not overcome him because he was walking with God. He said that God "restoreth my soul" (Ps. 23:3). If your soul has been restored to fellowship with God, you have true happiness.

The psalmist writes, "Thou preparest a table before me" (Ps. 23:5); he was enjoying spiritual food that others knew nothing about. "My cup runneth over" (Ps. 23:5); he had so much joy that he just couldn't keep it inside, so he shared it with others.

14

What Is Ecstasy?

He concluded this Psalm by declaring, "I will dwell in the house of the Lord for ever" (Ps. 23:6). Some folks desperately want to be happy for one night, but that is not enough. If you find the fullness of life, you will want it forever—and you can have it forever! God has promised it. This security is ecstasy.

Peace of Mind

When your soul is right with God, your entire being will be at peace. You will think and act in a positive, victorious way. You will have peace of mind.

Eugenia Price tells about being fired from her job as a radio announcer many years ago. As she walked out of her boss's office, she thought of the round-bottom wooden clowns she and her brother had as children. When they would hit the clowns with their fists, the clowns would rock over to one side and then stand up straight again.

The Lord seemed to be using this as a symbol in her own life. Problems might knock her over, but she could stand up straight again. "Then I thought how heart-breaking it would be to have been the poor man who had to fire me!" she writes. "For me this was not only a completely unusual reaction, but it warmed me in a strange and tender way...."[3] She had peace of mind.

God's Word tells us that the peace of God "surpasses all understanding" (Phil. 4:7). His peace is so marvelous and rich that it goes beyond our human way of thinking. He can solve problems and wipe away sorrows that seem past hope. The peace of mind that tells you God will find a way through your times of trouble is ecstasy.

Forgiveness

Many people do not know the ecstasy of being forgiven. But ask the prisoner who's been pardoned. He knows what it means to be happy! He does not deserve to go free, so when he walks through those iron doors for the last time, he is certainly a happy person.

Satan works overtime to try to make us doubt that we are forgiven. He tells us that we are not worth being forgiven. He makes fun of the way we repent, and he says, "You'll never succeed. You'll sin again. Then God will have no use for you."

But in God's Book we are *not* condemned; we are set free. Look what it says: "There is therefore now no condemnation to those who are in Christ Jesus, who do not walk according to the flesh, but according to the Spirit. For the law of the Spirit of life in Christ Jesus has made me free from the law of sin and death" (Rom. 8:1, 2). Read that last verse aloud: *For the . . . Spirit of life in Christ Jesus has made me free from the law of sin and death.* It's true! If you've surrendered your life to Jesus Christ, God has forgiven your sins. You're free from the death penalty of sin. *You're alive, and you're going to live forever.* Isn't that exciting? Doesn't it fill your heart with joy?

When you can say in all confidence, "God has pardoned all my sin," you will know pure ecstasy!

Absence of Fear

Fearful people are not happy. Some are afraid of the past; others are afraid of the future. Some

16

people tremble in fear of dogs or snakes or rats. Others are afraid of the dark. But many, many people—more than would ever admit it—are afraid of life itself. They are afraid that something they say or do will cost them their friends, their job, or their sense of self-worth. Most of all, they're afraid that their lives are traveling down a dead-end street and there's nothing they can do about it.

The monster of fear must be broken if you want to live a life of ecstasy. God can break that monster for you.

Scripture says that "God has not given us a spirit of fear but of power and of love and of a sound mind" (2 Tim. 1:7). You see, fear is not characteristic of a Christian; it indicates that one is not fully relying on God. A Christian should be able to face fearsome situations with confidence and control. When he can't, it's a signal that he's taking his life out of God's hands and trying to mold it with his own.

Francis and Edith Schaeffer were moving their family to Switzerland when polio struck their son, Franky. Francis was at a missionary conference in southern Italy, so Edith had to decide what to do. A Swiss doctor urged her to let him use an experimental drug on the young boy. He insisted that it must be given right away, and it had to be injected while Franky was under ether.

Edith prayed, "O Father, show me what is best for Franky. I'll go with the doctor unless you stop me, God. I don't know how else to do it." She let the doctor administer the drug.

Through the night she waited beside Franky's hospital bed, reading her Bible. She came across the verse that said, "The king's heart is in the hand of the Lord, as the rivers of water: he turneth it

17

whithersoever he will" (Prov. 21:1). Suddenly she realized that she didn't need to be afraid; if God could guide the heart of a king, he could surely guide the heart of a doctor! As she asked God to do this, she relaxed and her fears faded away.

The next morning the doctor decided not to give Franky any more shots. The boy recovered.[4]

You will face some frightening situations in your life, but you have no need to be afraid. You can put your confidence in God. You can lick fear, and that brings ecstasy.

Fellowship and Acceptance

Since ecstasy comes from a proper relationship with God, a person who is hostile toward God can never be truly happy. But happiness is also based upon a healthy relationship with other people. So if you are going to fight your family and your fellowman, you are not going to be happy. Simply put, ecstasy means fellowship with God *and* with your fellowman.

Ecstasy also means having a good relationship with yourself. It means a life of inner peace that unifies your soul with all of your being. It means being at home with yourself—being happy with yourself, regardless of what you have been or what you may become. Paul said, "I have learned in whatever state I am, to be content" (Phil. 4:11). When you master this art of self-acceptance, you will be happy.

So what is ecstasy? It is contentment, security, peace of mind, a sense of forgiveness, and living a life without fear. Ecstasy is tremendous spiritual energy that enlivens every part of your being. When you have ecstasy, your spirit tells your mind, "Be happy!" It tells your emotions, "Sing out!" It causes your heart to say, "Not my will, but Thine be done."

A person who has ecstasy can harness the boundless spiritual energy that comes from God, so that it changes the emotional climate in which he lives. People can see a difference in this person. He's happy, helpful, and hopeful about the future. So they begin to change the way they act toward him; they begin to reflect what they see in this ecstatic Christian's face.

The Bible says that the kingdom of God is "righteousness and peace and joy in the Holy Spirit" (Rom. 14:17). Joy! It's the divine joy that comes when we are born again through Jesus Christ. But the Bible also says, "The joy of the Lord is your strength" (Neh. 8:10). It's divine power—the power to heal, to cast out demons, to preach good news to the poor. Ecstasy is God-given, contagious energy. It comes to a life totally yielded to the will of God.

God's ecstasy can be yours right now. You can turn from sadness to gladness by the power of the Lord Jesus Christ.

II
What Is Man?

When I consider thy heavens,
the work of thy fingers,
the moon and the stars,
which thou hast ordained;
What is man, that thou art
mindful of him?
and the son of man, that
thou visitest him?

—Psalm 8:3,4

Each of us lives in three dimensions. The human personality has three distinct components, and they all must function in harmony if a person is to be happy. These three aspects of the personality are the *spirit,* the *soul,* and the *body.*

Paul identified these components in his first letter to the Thessalonians when he said, "May the God of peace Himself sanctify you completely; and may your whole spirit, soul, and body be preserved blameless at the coming of our Lord Jesus Christ" (1 Thess. 5:23).

In order to understand how a person finds ecstasy, we need to study these three dimensions of the personality. This study will reveal the problems encountered when a person lives a disjointed life, with the three aspects of his nature at odds with one another. It will also show that God intends for us to be whole, harmonious persons.

The Soul

Your *soul* is your human nature, your creatureliness, the sum of the qualities that identify you as a human being. The Bible says that "the Lord God formed man of the dust of the ground, and breathed into his nostrils the breath of life; and man became a living soul" (Gen. 2:7). The Hebrew word for "soul" literally means "created life." Unlike the life of the Creator, man's life has a moment of beginning—the moment God creates it. So man's soul reflects the life-force of God. But it is only a reflection: It has not existed forever; it cannot create other souls; and it cannot continue to exist if God chooses to snuff it out.

Imagine that your soul is a mirror. God's Spirit is the face of the craftsman who made the mirror. The mirror exists because the craftsman made it; in the same way, you exist because God created you. The mirror *is* a mirror because the craftsman is able to see himself in it; and you are genuinely human when you reflect the "image of God" that you were meant to reflect. To the extent that your personality reflects God's personality, you are a human being. This human identity is what we call the *soul*.

In a way, the soul is independent of God because it makes its own choices. At the same time, it is dependent upon God because God created it and gives it the freedom to act. It is like an airplane that soars and loops through the air, seeming perfectly free but depending on the buoyancy of the air to keep it aloft.

Your soul is your humanness; willful and rebellious though it may be, your humanness comes from God. When your soul strays from God, you become less human. So at the very core of our personalities, we need God. The evangelist Billy Graham has observed:

> The soul ... demands fellowship and communion with God. It demands worship, quietness, and meditation.... The soul was made for God, and without God it is restless and in secret torment.[1]

At some time or another, everyone has felt an inner emptiness, a sense of worthlessness, which is the sign of soul hunger. It means that you need to focus your entire being upon serving God and honoring Him. If you do anything less, you are cheating your soul—your own identity—of the purpose for which it was created.

Soul satisfaction comes from reflecting in your own life the qualities of God. It comes from living as a child of God, with a family resemblance to the Creator.

Before I gave my life to God, I knew I was deceiving the people around me. I pretended to be whatever I needed to be to fit in with the groups of people I admired. I was a vile, vulgar person with my street friends, but a very proper, well-mannered person with my parents. Every night I faced Lester Sumrall in the mirror and all my evil words came back to haunt me. I was a misfit. I was uneasy with my friends, uneasy with my parents, and uneasy in the sight of God. My soul was not right with God. I was sullen, dejected, and bitter.

At last I gave myself to God. I placed my life back in His hands, and He cleansed me of my ungodly ways. I went to the people I had cursed and condemned, and I asked them to forgive me for what I had done. That brought peace to my heart and ecstasy to my entire life. I began to love others as God loved me, and my soul found the purpose God had intended for it. Everyone can have this kind of deep contentment and joy.

The Body

We neglect the body, perhaps more than we neglect any other component of our personal makeup. Yet God created our bodies, just as He made our souls and spirits. He has a purpose for our bodies, and if we ignore that purpose we sin against God.

The body is your physical form. Scripture says that "the Lord God formed man of the dust of the ground" (Gen. 2:7). Dust and all the other physical things of this world are not repulsive to Him; He made them! And the body is not repulsive to God, for He made it as lovingly and carefully as He made the majestic Rocky Mountains and the great Pacific Ocean. The poet James Weldon Johnson has written:

> . . . The great God Almighty
> Who lit the sun and fixed it in the sky,
> Who flung the stars to the most far corner
>   of the night,
> Who rounded the earth in the middle of his hand;

24

What Is Man?

This Great God,
Like a mammy bending over her baby,
Kneeled down in the dust
Toiling over a lump of clay
Till he shaped it in his own image. . . .[2]

That's just how the Bible describes the creation of the body: God lovingly made it to perform all the tasks He intended His children to do in this world. He wants us to have healthy, whole bodies to serve Him.

But often we Americans abuse our bodies. We get tense, anxious, and overwrought. We eat junk foods that make us flabby and weak. We expose ourselves to disease and disability by smoking cigarettes, by overeating, by taking drugs, or by indulging in promiscuous sex. This ruins the bodies God created for us. When the body is "all messed up" because of neglect and abuse, it is difficult to know the ecstasy of living in fellowship with God.

God can heal broken bodies. That in itself shows how important He considers the body to be. He can restore disabled arms and legs, bring sight to blind eyes, and rid the body of cancer or any other dread disease. He does not always choose to bring physical healing, but hundreds of thousands of people will testify that He has healed them. Obviously, He values the bodies He gave us.

Many years ago, a Canadian man named Henry Harvey agonized over his wife's incurable disease. A man at the factory where he worked suggested that they take her to a gospel tent meeting on the outskirts of town, where his aunt had been healed of cancer a week before. Henry was doubtful. But that night, as he and his wife were reading the Bible in their regular devotions, they came to Romans

8:11; "He who raised Christ from the dead will also give life to your mortal bodies by His Spirit who dwells in you."

"That's strange," Henry said, "I always thought that verse referred to our spirits or souls. But it says God will quicken our *mortal* bodies."

This confused him, because he had been taught that God no longer performed healing miracles. But after he prayed for God's guidance and meditated on that Scripture verse, Henry took his wife to see the evangelist. The preacher shared with her several Bible passages about healing and prayed with her.

But a week later she started to hemorrhage again. They decided not call the doctor and to pray instead. She began to improve that very night. In fact, she later bore another son, Richard, who became a leading evangelist with the Christian and Missionary Alliance. She lived to be eighty-one years old.[3]

God cares for our mortal bodies because they are a vital aspect of our being.

The Spirit

Hundreds of people come into my study for counseling every year, and their most common problems are spiritual. Husbands say, "She won't worship with me." Wives say, "He doesn't love God." Many, many people have fallen into divorce and an untold number of problems because they had trouble of the spirit.

The *spirit* is the God-sensitive aspect of the human personality. The psalmist said, "Create in me a clean heart, O God; and renew a right spirit within me" (Ps. 51:10). He knew that his spirit could hear God even when his soul was distracted by sin. We might say one's spirit is the rudder God uses to steer one's life toward Him.

The spirit is like an antenna that receives impulses of the Father's will. A radio antenna receives signals twenty-four hours a day, but we hear them only when we turn on the receiver and tune to the station we are seeking. In much the same way, the human spirit is always aware of God's will, but we may not realize it because we ignore this component of the self.

As Christians, our spirits within us assure us that our sins have been forgiven and we belong to God. When a person hears the gospel, his spirit rejoices within him because the message confirms what the spirit has sensed all along. When you heed what your spirit tells you and accept the truth of Christ, you open the door to a life of happiness and delight—a life of ecstasy!

The writer of Proverbs says, "The spirit of man is the candle of the Lord, searching all the inward parts of the belly" (Prov. 20:27). Here we have a clear picture of the spirit and its function. It is the "candle of the Lord," illuminating the deep recesses of the human mind. An old Greek philosopher, Diogenes, walked the streets with a lantern, searching for an honest man. Similarly, the human spirit is searching for an honest response to the gospel. Sometimes the soul responds; often it does not.

Notice what happens to the spirit when the body dies. The Bible says, "Then shall the dust return to the earth as it was: and the spirit shall return unto God who gave it" (Eccl. 12:7). The body is temporal;

it will grow old and die. But your spirit does not die, and when your physical life is ended your spirit will return to God.

Many people use the words *spirit* and *soul* interchangeably, as if the words refer to the same thing. But those who do this misunderstand the nature of these two important facets of the human personality. Both the spirit and the soul are invisible, and both live after the body dies. But there the similarity stops.

The soul is *created* by God; it is the unique package of human characteristics that is "you." The spirit is *given* by God to aid your soul; we might say it is your soul's window on heaven. The spirit is subject to the decisions of your mind and the inclinations of your soul, so it may be disregarded altogether. But if you do this, you wreck the destiny of your soul. For just as the divine spirit within you returns to God when you die, your soul will stand before God on Judgment Day. Then you—your soul—must give account for what you have done with your life. If you've ignored your spirit and wasted your life in sinning against God, you will be punished. Jesus said that Satan "is able to destroy both soul and body in hell" (Matt. 10:28); and the prophet Ezekiel warned, "The soul that sinneth, it shall die" (Ezek. 18:20).

But if the soul chooses to serve God, it finds ecstasy in life here and now, and the prospect of happiness forever. Even the sorrowing sage who wrote Lamentations knew that this was so. "The Lord is my portion, saith my soul; therefore will I hope in him. The Lord is good unto them that wait for him, to the soul that seeketh him" (Lam. 3:24,25).

So we see that the soul has the power of choice. If

it uses that power wisely and chooses to serve the Master of life, it will be joyfully rewarded.

Holy Harmony

The total human person—spirit, soul, and body—must be what God wants it to be. When all components of the personality work together in serving the Lord, the individual will be happy. That's how God meant for us to live. When a person's spirit rules his life, the facts that the mind perceives will filter through the spirit into the soul and body. God communicates with the spirit; the spirit guides the mind; and the mind directs the body. When the personality is so ordered, it is harmonious and happy.

Have you ever watched a football team in spring training camp? Usually the line is full of fresh recruits, men who are not accustomed to playing together. Now football players are not supermen; each one has certain strengths and weaknesses. So a seasoned team makes the best of its players' strengths and covers for their weaknesses. But a team in spring training can't do that. The players don't know what to expect of each other. So they miss each other's signals. They leave gaps in their defense. They fumble the ball.

Many people go through life that way. They're always in "spring training." They don't make the three components of their personality work together. So the soul misses signals from the spirit; the body charges ahead of the soul; and the person makes an utter mess of his life.

It doesn't have to be that way. Christ can coordi-

nate all three members of our personal "team." He
can train them to work together and set their sights
on the goal of eternal life. When our personalities
have this holy harmony, we will feel ecstasy
throughout our beings.

Of course, we must cooperate with Christ in this
process. We must discipline ourselves to heed our
spirits' guidance. We must conform our souls to the
godly nature that the Holy Spirit reveals to our
spirits. And we must keep our bodies pure and
strong to do what Christ wants us to do. This uni-
fied vision of the self should guide every facet of
our lives.

I often tell young people who are contemplating
marriage that there are three ways to be married.

First, they can be married in *body*. Millions of
people marry simply to gratify their sexual appetites; they want to enjoy someone else's body. They
soon tire of this and look for a divorce court, so they
can be free to try yet another body. Physical marriage isn't all there is to marriage, even though it's
an important part.

Second, they can be married in *soul*. They may
say to one another, "I like your way of thinking," or
"You respond to things the way I do," or "We seem
very compatible." Such couples have a better understanding of one another, and they are more
likely to have a successful marriage. But again, this
is only a part of what marriage should be.

Third, they can be married in *spirit*. As I mentioned before, many people who come to me for
counseling have spiritual problems, and I have
seen many marriages ruined by spiritual conflict.
Christians who try to be "unequally yoked together

with unbelievers" are headed for heartbreak (cf. 2 Cor. 6:14).

A couple should marry in all three ways, and they should start with the realm of the spirit. If your sweetheart is indifferent toward God and feels uncomfortable about going to church with you, it's time to cool the romance. But if you are together in spirit, soul, and body, you ought to praise the Lord! A threefold cord is not easily broken, and a three-way marriage is sure to be happy.

To find ecstasy, a person needs to have a proper relationship with God, a proper relationship with his fellowman, and a proper relationship with himself. You have seen how to bring order and harmony to your inner being, to "yourself." Now let us see how to establish a proper link with God, the Giver of ecstasy.

III

The Birth of Ecstasy

Turn your eyes upon Jesus,
  Look full in His wonderful face,
And the things of earth will grow strangely dim
  In the light of His glory and grace.

—Helen H. Lemmel*

Have you ever drilled for water? If you have, you know that deep underground there is a reservoir of water called the "water table." If you drill to the proper depth, you can tap into it. This reservoir rises and falls with periods of rain and drought. Sometimes the water table is so high that it squirts water through a crack in a rock formation. Sometimes it sinks so low that your well dries up and you need to drill deeper. But the water is always there somewhere.

The same is true of ecstasy. It is always available, free for the asking, but sometimes we don't know where or how to find it.

Job was afflicted by all kinds of troubles and hardships, and he asked God why he had to suffer these things. Job said, "The days of affliction have taken hold upon me" (Job 30:16).

Notice God's reply: "Where wast thou when I laid the foundations of the earth? . . . When the morning stars sang together, and all the sons of God shouted for joy?" (Job 38:4,7). In other words, God was telling Job not to question His way of doing things.

But notice what else God said here: When He created the earth, "all the sons of God shouted for joy." That means *there has been joy since the very first day of creation,* even before man was created! When Job moaned about his "days of affliction," God reminded him that joy had always been available. Even when life is the gloomiest, hope and happiness are waiting just offstage, ready for us to summon them. In this chapter we will see how to tap into God's reservoir of joy.

I began to experience true joy at the moment of my conversion to Jesus Christ. Before that, I did not have the happiness we have been talking about. I was full of remorse, sadness, anger, and hate. I was sullen and belligerent. Real joy came only when I was "born again" by the Spirit of God; ecstasy came by the blood of Jesus when I was saved.

First Peter 2:9 says, "You are a chosen generation, a royal priesthood, a holy nation, His own special people, that you may proclaim the praises of Him who has called you out of darkness into His marvelous light." Just think of it! As a believer, I am a *chosen* person; God chose me to have a blood relationship with the Most High! I have moved from the darkness of being spiritually lost to the light of His glorious presence. I am now united with Him. This is how ecstasy begins.

Harold Lindsell, a leading evangelical writer,

made this perceptive comment in his book *The World, the Flesh, and the Devil:*

> Man's greatest problem has never been one of environment in the form of food, shelter, or clothing. It has never been that of human estrangement, racial strife, or economic inequality. Man's greatest problem has been his alienation from God. He was made in God's image, rooted and grounded in God, and when man lost God he lost himself.[1]

Alienation from God—this is the root of the world's unhappiness. We may blame it on our lack of money, our lack of education, or even our lack of gasoline! But when you peel back all the pretensions and excuses, you find that unhappiness comes from sin. It's a signal that we have cut ourselves off from God. And the only real cure for unhappiness is to turn back to God, to repent of our sins.

The Jailer's Experience

Consider the jailer at Philippi (Acts 16:23–34). Here was a man with a very responsible office in Roman government. He respected the chain of command (v. 24), and we assume that he received a decent salary. Then an earthquake rocked the jail and loosened the prisoners' bonds—but they didn't escape. We might think the jailer was very fortunate. But was he happy? No! He ran into the cell of Paul and Silas, fell on his knees, and cried, "Sirs, what must I do to be saved?" (Acts 16:30). His close brush with death made him realize how unpredictable life is. He could die at any moment, so how could he be happy?

35

Paul and Silas could have said, "Find a job that's less risky." Or, "Move to the country and try the simple life." Or, "Take up the study of philosophy." But none of those answers would have gotten to the bottom of the jailer's problem. He had cut himself off from God, and he could not be content until he returned. So Paul and Silas said, "Believe on the Lord Jesus Christ, and you will be saved" (Acts 16:31).

He took their advice. He surrendered his life to the Lord and was baptized that very night. "And when he had brought them into his house," the Bible says, "he set food before them; and he rejoiced, believing in God with all his household" (Acts 16:34). That's the picture of a happy man.

Salvation through Christ brings happiness. Fellowship with God *is* happiness. "Whoso trusteth in the Lord, happy is he" (Prov. 16:20). "For we ... who worship God in the Spirit, rejoice in Christ Jesus, and have no confidence in the flesh" (Phil. 3:3). "Though now you do not see Him, yet believing, you rejoice with joy unspeakable and full of glory, receiving the end of your faith—the salvation of your souls" (1 Pet. 1:8,9).

Ecstasy comes into our lives when Christ comes into our lives.

Happy to Suffer

Christianity was not very popular in the days of the apostles. Respectable people looked down their noses at the zealous folks who worshiped this man the Romans had crucified. Yet the Christians stayed true to their Lord. They kept on meeting together, studying the Scriptures, and preaching.

Finally, the high Jewish court brought the apostles to trial. The Pharisees proudly pulled their robes around them and rebuked the Jesus-followers. Then they ordered their servants to beat the evangelists and warned the bleeding men to stop preaching.

So what do you suppose the apostles did? Cry on each others' shoulders? No! The Bible says, "They departed from the presence of the council, rejoicing that they were counted worthy to suffer shame for His name" (Acts 5:41). They rejoiced! They were happy—not because they were comfortable, or rich, or famous—but because they were serving the Lord.

The Joy of Forgiveness

What kind of joy does Christ bring? For one thing, He brings the joy of knowing that your sins are forgiven. Everyone longs to be free from the guilt of wrongdoing; everyone wants to face the future without fearing that God will punish him. And everyone can! Jesus gave His life on Calvary to guarantee it. He has paid the price for our sins, and each of us can claim the freedom from sin that He's made available.

One day the Pharisees brought to Jesus a woman they had caught in the act of adultery. They wanted to test Jesus. They knew He preached forgiveness and love, and yet the Law stated that a woman caught in adultery should receive the death penalty. Which would Jesus follow—the Law or this gospel of His own? "What do You say?" they asked (John 8:5).

Jesus ignored their question, so they asked Him

again. They badgered Him for an answer. At last He stood up and said, "He who is without sin among you, let him throw a stone at her first" (John 8:7). No one dared to claim that he was sinless, so one by one they shuffled away.

Then Jesus asked the adulteress, "Woman, where are those accusers of yours? Has no one condemned you?"

She said, "No one, Lord."

"Neither do I condemn you," Jesus said. "Go and sin no more" (John 8:10,11). This is a gripping story of the forgiveness Christ offers all of us.

But don't stop here. Read the next verse: "Then Jesus spoke to them again, saying, 'I am the light of the world. He who follows Me shall not walk in darkness, but have the light of life' " (John 8:12). Jesus says His forgiveness brings light into the world. It dispels the darkness of sin and guilt; it can give every individual a clear vision of God and His love. That's exciting!

When a person accepts God's forgiveness, he naturally becomes more forgiving toward others. He passes on the mercy God has given him. Like a modern chorus says, "You spread His love to everyone; you want to pass it on." That's the beauty of forgiveness.

John Wesley said, "If I have any strength, it is the power to forgive." That's true of every one of us. Some may think a forgiving attitude is a sign of weakness or naiveté, but God doesn't. It is one of the outstanding characteristics of His own personality. You should be able to pardon the hurt someone has inflicted upon you. Humanly, that's very difficult to do; but with God all things are possible—even forgiveness.

The Birth of Ecstasy

Peter Marshall, a former chaplain of the U.S. Senate, used to pray: "Lord, where we are wrong, make us willing to change, and where we are right, make us easy to live with. . . ."

That's the spirit of forgiveness. If you spend many years in the Christian life, you will learn that the most forgiving people are the happiest people.

The Joy of Fellowship

Christ brings *the joy of His companionship*. When you accept Him as the Lord of your life, you find that He goes with you through every experience of every day. When your friends praise you and honor you, Christ is there beside you. When it seems that everyone rejects you, He's still there. You can talk with Him and "[cast] all your care upon Him" (1 Pet. 5:7). As I once heard someone say, "The Lord doesn't promise that your car will never break down; but if it does, He'll wait with you till the wrecker comes." His companionship can make all the difference in your attitude toward life.

Scientists who planned spaceflights to the moon wondered how the astronauts would react to total isolation. Each man who stayed in the capsule orbiting the moon spent half his time on the dark side, out of communication with those on earth. He was alone in a way no one had ever been before. He had no other human being to talk with, no familiar landmarks to see, not even a way to signal for help. Yet these astronauts did not panic. They were so awed by the sight of the moon that all thoughts of fear vanished. They were peaceful, confident, and exhilarated as they meditated upon that spectacle.

I think this is the key to the problem of loneliness. We feel lonely when we get so caught up in our everyday problems that we forget the God who watches over us all. If we would realize that God is here, caring about everything that happens to us, we would not feel lonely. We would be so awed by the unfolding drama of our lives, with all its complications and questions, that we would never pause to feel lonely.

When Ney Bailey joined the staff of Campus Crusade for Christ, she was sent to begin a Campus Crusade program at the University of Arizona, in Tucson. Just after she arrived, the two men who were supposed to "show her the ropes" had to leave on urgent business, so Ney was left in a strange city, with no friends, facing a difficult job. She wanted to quit and go home. Over Christmas vacation she went back to Louisiana to attend a friend's wedding and toyed with the idea of staying there. But she reminded herself there were only five more months in the school term; surely she could tough it out that long.

But God had other plans for Ney. When she arrived back in Tucson she had received a letter from a friend in Hawaii, who encouraged her to hear a certain evangelist who was going to speak in Phoenix. Ney decided to go, and she was surprised to hear the speaker announce that the topic of his message for that evening was "Defeated Christians."

"I listened as if I were the only person in the room," Ney writes. "He spoke of trying to live the Christian life on one's own resources, through self-effort. And he remarked that God often allows failure—to point us to one crucial truth: that we cannot live the Christian life on our own."

Ney certainly felt like a failure, and as she listened to the message she realized that she had tried to handle the Campus Crusade assignment on her own. That was impossible. She needed the Lord's companionship.

"If you want to live for Jesus Christ this year and the rest of your life," the evangelist said, "and if you want Jesus Christ to begin to live through you, I want you to stand."

Ney stood.

"In that moment I surrendered my will, and my whole being, into the control of the Lord Jesus Christ," Ney says. "The Lord's presence became as real to me as when I first trusted Him as Savior."[2]

Can you say that of your relationship with the Lord? Do you feel Him with you just as much as you did when you first became a Christian? Don't miss the joy of His fellowship.

The Joy of Witnessing

Most important, Christ brings *the joy of leading others to Him*. You may be saying, "What? How can that be a joy? I'm scared about witnessing to other people." But it *is* a joy to tell others what the Lord means to you. It made the apostles so happy that, after the Jewish council punished them, they could hardly wait to get out on the streets and start preaching again!

Not every Christian has to preach. But when the Lord comes into your life you'll get so excited about Him that you'll start to share Him somehow—in spite of your shyness.

A great preacher of the nineteenth century, O. P. Gifford, spoke to his Boston congregation one

Sunday on the importance of soul-winning. He declared that witnessing ought to be the Christian's first order of business, and no one should let a day pass without sharing Christ with someone else. He closed his sermon by saying, "Every Christian can win somebody to Christ."

As the congregation filed out, a poor seamstress lingered behind. She finally confronted the preacher and said, "Pastor, this is the first time I've heard you say something unfair."

"How have I been unfair?" Pastor Gifford asked.

"You kept saying that every Christian could win somebody to Christ, and you made no exceptions. But surely I am an exception. How could I win somebody to Christ? I'm only a poor sewing lady, and I work from daylight till dark just to feed my family. I have no education and no opportunity to visit the unsaved, and yet you seem to think that I can lead someone to the Lord. You've not been fair."

The pastor took her hand and looked earnestly into her eyes. "Tell me," he said, "does anyone ever come to your house?"

"Why, certainly, a few people come there."

"Does the milkman come?"

"To be sure," the woman said with a puzzled look. "He comes every morning."

"And how about the bread man? Does he come to your door?"

"To be sure. He comes every day."

The pastor waited a moment and then simply said, "A word to the wise is sufficient."

The old woman went home and pondered this. She gradually realized that she had plenty of opportunities to tell others about Christ every day. She resolved to begin right away.

The next morning she got up bright and early to meet the milkman. He was surprised to see her at that hour, and she mumbled a lame excuse about having a lot of work to do that day. The milkman turned and went out the gate.

"Wait a minute!" the woman shouted. "I have something to say to you!"

The milkman came back.

With tears streaming down her face, she said, "Do you know Christ? Are you a Christian?"

The milkman nearly dropped his basket. He told her that he had not been able to sleep for the past two nights because he felt under the conviction of his sin. "If you know how to find the light," he said, "you're the person I need to talk to."

So there on the stoop of her Boston row house the seamstress told how she had become a Christian. She did not know any "spiritual laws" to share with him, or even any Scripture verses to drive the story home. But she did know what a change Christ had brought to her life, and that's what she told the milkman. He accepted Christ, too.

Sharing Christ is the most thrilling experience you'll ever have. And it's just a part of the joy Christ can bring to your life.

IV

How to Nourish the Gift

[The Christian] sometimes does most by doing nothing and goes furthest when standing still. In heaviness he manages to rejoice and keeps his heart glad even in sorrow.

—A. W. Tozer[1]

Unless we protect and nourish this gift of joy, we will lose it. We must keep on renewing our relationship with God through Christ. Otherwise it will become as cold and joyless as a marriage where the partners have stopped saying, "I love you." Let us consider some ways to keep this relationship fresh and ecstatically joyful.

Solitude

When people see me in public (whether speaking before a live audience or communicating with TV viewers), they think I am a happy person. And I *am* happy. It's not an act that I put on for the camera; I am truly a joyful person. But I must confess that I am happiest when I am alone, because then I can have direct, uninterrupted communion with the Lord.

I like to sit in my study, away from the jingling of telephones and the tensions of everyday business. In the study I have a collection of mementos from around the world—personal items that remind me of the wonderful experiences God has given me. I love to ponder these souvenirs of my ministry. My inner being sings to God and I rejoice in these times. It's my way of taking a fresh bucketful from the well of happiness.

I'm not the only person who does this. Charles L. Allen, a distinguished radio minister, gives this advice to people who have lost contact with God:

> I have said to many people in "the valley of the shadow" to get off by themselves in a quiet place. Quit struggling for a little while. Forget the many details. Stop your mind for a little while from hurrying on to the morrow and to next year and beyond.
>
> Just stop, become still and quiet, and in the midst of your "glen of gloom" you will feel a strange and marvelous presence more powerfully than you have ever felt it before. . . . There is power in "His presence."[2]

Indeed there is! As I sit alone in my study and pour out my heart to God, He gives me certain divine enablements that I'm sure I could not receive in any other way. He reveals answers to problems that seem beyond solving. He teaches me the deep, deep truths of His love. He gives me spiritual gifts I could not attain through my own striving. Deep within my inner self there flows a perpetual happiness; every fiber of my being tingles with ecstasy. I have it!

How to Nourish the Gift

"But," you may say, "Lester Sumrall must have troubles too!" I certainly do. But beneath them flows this sense of blessing that I am talking about. Even in my troubles I have peace—a peace I find by taking time to be alone with my Lord.

When I was in Norway, a tour guide kept calling me "Mister All Summer."

I laughed and said, "Well, that sounds all right because all summer is in my heart."

"What do you mean?" the guide asked.

"I mean the Sun of Righteousness lives there," I said. "He's shining every day."

In my times of solitude I have a positive relationship with the Creator of the universe. These times of spiritual communion are the most satisfying experiences I have ever known. I want you to have this ecstasy for yourself on a daily, hourly basis. And I firmly believe that taking time to be alone with God is the first step toward finding it.

In Psalm 46, we find a description of the many horrible calamities that plague the earth. Warfare, earthquake, flood—they march past us in ghastly array. Then we come to verse 10 and read, "Be still, and know that I am God: I will be exalted among the heathen, I will be exalted in the earth."

In the midst of all our troubles, we need to be still and realize that God is in control. We need to reorient ourselves to Him again and again as we grapple with our problems.

In the early days of radio, before we had transistors or even vacuum tubes, receivers were tuned by using a small rock crystal and a wire filament called a "cat whisker." Radio engineers had learned that rock crystals vibrate thousands of times each second, and by placing the cat whisker at just the right spot on the crystal, a listener could find the frequency of the station he wanted to hear.

Of course, he had to be careful not to bump the radio set after he found the station or the cat whisker would slip from the proper place on the crystal and he would have to search for the station again. Even the rumbling of a heavy truck on a nearby street could jiggle the cat whisker off its target. So it was best to keep the radio set on a heavy wooden table that would resist the bumps and jars of the household.

Your spirit is just as sensitive as that old-fashioned radio. If you want to get "tuned in" to God and really concentrate on what He's trying to tell you, spend some time in quiet meditation. Be still and know Him.

Trust

We need to claim what is ours. You see, ecstasy is a sacred gift. It comes from God, it is intended to bless God's people, and it should be used to glorify Him. We cannot earn or deserve ecstasy, but we must claim it. F. B. Meyer said, "Some people are always telegraphing to heaven for God to send a cargo of blessing to them, but they are not at the wharf-side to unload the vessel when it comes. How many of God's richest blessings . . . have come right close to you, but you do not know how to lay hold of and use them."[3]

Many people beg God to bring peace to their hearts when God has already granted them that gift. Like Job, they are so busy wringing their hands, thumping their chests, and moaning about their predicaments that they don't realize they are in the presence of God the Almighty. Like Martha, they are so anxious to see that their table is set that they ignore the Holy Guest who is at the table. They need to step back from their predicament and let God show them how it looks from His point of view.

If you hire a contractor to build a house, you might require him to give you a "performance bond." This document guarantees that the contractor will complete his work by a certain date. If he fails to do so, or if he "skips town" altogether, you can collect damages from the company that posted the bond. It's the safe way to build.

Many people want to build their lives the same way, and they want God to give them a performance bond before they begin. They've heard His promises of happiness and heaven, but they want to be on the safe side. So they hold their lives back from Him pending more proof of what He said.

This is where trust is needed. When a person steps out in faith every day, believing that God will do what He has promised, he will find that God's goodness is "new every morning" (Lam. 3:23).

I know it's hard to trust the Lord when your friends ridicule you for doing it. Yet that's the only way to keep your faith alive. Keep on believing God's promises when everything else seems to contradict them, and you'll be far happier than the skeptics who try to beat you down. Skeptics may congratulate themselves for being "realistic," but self-praise is as close as they come to being happy.

Humility and Poise

Several years ago, the editor of a large Christian magazine received a fiery letter from one of his readers who was complaining about the stands the editor was taking on certain controversial issues. The reader ended his attack by saying, "If you don't straighten up I'm going to cancel my subscription!"

The editor read the letter, picked up his pen, and wrote a single word in large letters across the bottom: "RELAX." Then he mailed the letter back.

A few days later the editor got another letter from his irate reader. He opened the envelope and found a sheet of paper with the word: "RELAXED!"

That's the kind of attitude we need in order to cultivate ecstasy. The Bible says, "Therefore humble yourselves under the mighty hand of God, that He may exalt you in due time, casting all your care upon Him, for He cares for you" (1 Pet. 5:6,7). Do you want to be "exalted," lifted up from disappointment and despair? Then humble yourself under the mighty hand of God. Instead of focusing on *your* problem, *your* weakness, and *your* hurt feelings, focus on *His* wisdom, *His* power, and *His* love and comfort. Give your troubles to Him. Trust Him to take care of them. That's how you put yourself under His mighty hand.

Think of the most humble Christian you know. It may be your pastor, your Sunday school teacher, your mother or father, or someone who works with you at the plant or office. Fix that person's face in your mind. Now ask yourself: *Is this person weaker or stronger for being humble?* The answer may surprise you!

Corrie ten Boom is one of the most humble Christian people I know, yet God has used her mightily. She has reached millions of people through her books, her spoken messages, and her movies. If you've ever seen Corrie in person, you know that she radiates happiness with every fiber of her being. Her face, her gestures, and even her walk exude an unusual vitality for someone her age. She has found her own "fountain of youth" by submitting her life to the Lord day after day.

Corrie has endured the suffering of Nazi concentration camps, the disappointments of the ministry, the discouragement of trying to finance a prison ministry and a dozen other projects. But when troubles and disappointments come, she does not take them personally. She surrenders them to the Lord, because she knows her entire life and ministry are His.

She has what I like to call a "holy nonchalance" about what she's doing. It's not that she doesn't care about what happens; she cares intensely. But she has no anxiety about her work, because she leaves it all in her heavenly Father's hands.

Prayer

The spiritual communication of prayer is the most satisfying experience we can have on this planet, and it is vital for renewing the ecstasy of the Christian life. Remember that ecstasy is a divine quality, above and beyond humanity, transmitted to us by God Himself. So we must allow God to communicate with us every day if we want to be happy.

I have found that my secret prayer—prayer to God in private—brings such ecstasy that I often laugh while I am praying! Many people are not able to do that. But earnest prayer will bring joy into your life; it will show you that "his compassions fail not. They are new every morning" (Lam. 3:22,23). Your prayers will flow from the melody and praise of your inner being and fly directly to God.

Ecstasy: Finding Joy in Living

The Bible mentions "importunate" prayer, and many Christians are accustomed to this kind of praying. Webster defines "importunate" as "troublesomely urgent; overly persistent in request or demand." I'm sure you've had occasion to pray this way. You've pleaded with God to solve a particularly urgent problem; perhaps you've even fasted and locked yourself in your room for several hours to "pray through" the crisis. This kind of prayer is biblically sound and certainly necessary at times, but it is not the way a Christian should normally pray.

When Paul exhorted his Christian friends to pray, he described prayer as a joyful, thankful experience. He said:

> Rejoice always; pray without ceasing; in everything give thanks; for this is the will of God in Christ Jesus for you (1 Thess. 5:16–18).

> Therefore I desire that the men pray everywhere, lifting up holy hands, without wrath and doubting (1 Tim. 2:8).

The Book of Revelation says that the prayers of the saints are "incense"—a sweet-smelling fragrance that ascends to please God (Rev. 5:8; 8:3,4). Prayer is the spontaneous overflowing of a happy heart. Open the floodgate of joyful prayer each day, and God will keep filling your spiritual reservoir with ecstasy.

Bible Reading

I am very happy when I am reading and studying the Word of God. The psalmist said, "Thy word is a lamp unto my feet, and a light unto my path" (Ps. 119:105). That is certainly true in the Christian life. Reading the Bible brings light to our souls; it does something very beautiful and wonderful to the inner person.

I'm afraid that people who read silly novels, pornographic literature, and magazines filled with nonsense do not have ecstasy. They want to be happy, but they do not feast and drink from the Word of God.

"Since what we read in a real sense enters the soul," A. W. Tozer has said, "it is vitally important that we read the best and nothing but the best."[4]

The Bible is the Book of books. It contains the truth God has given us through inspired writers such as Isaiah, John, and Paul. In its pages we experience their joys and sorrows, we learn the lessons they learned firsthand, and we glimpse their vision of eternity. If no other book had ever been published and we had to rely on the Bible for our knowledge about how to live, it would be more than enough.

We can spend years studying the Scriptures and still be only novices. Every time I read Psalm 23 or the Sermon on the Mount I find new insights. The entire Bible is like that. It is a constant fountain of truth.

There is more than one way to study the Bible; many people give up reading it because they try only one or two ways. Don't be afraid to experiment! Even if you're satisfied with your Bible study habits, try a new approach once in a while, just to see what you find.

You may like a *doctrinal* approach. This method attempts to trace what the different Books of the Bible say about the central teachings of the Christian faith. Pick a doctrine you wish to study—redemption, for example—and use a concordance to find the verses that mention this doctrine. Make notes as you read. Write out the verses that strike you as being especially memorable. When you've finished, review your notes to see what the Bible says about this doctrine, from Genesis to Revelation. You might even decide to memorize some of the verses.

Another interesting approach to Bible study is the *thematic* method. Take a book of the Bible and attempt to identify the theme or themes the writer is dealing with. Don't consult any reference books to help you; see for yourself what the book has to say. Does it raise a question? Make an observation? Issue a prophecy? Declare a fact? When you've discerned the theme of the book, all of its parts will come into perspective like the intricate hues of a beautiful painting.

Perhaps you would like to try some *experiential* Bible study. Put yourself in the place of Joseph, Joshua, Esther, or some other biblical person. Read the Bible as if you are in the middle of the action. How do you feel when the Philistines send Goliath out against you? When the king throws you into the lion's den? When Jesus heals your crippled legs? Use your imagination. Let God stir your heart, like He stirred those of His children long ago.

If you are really interested in studying the Bible, and if you're willing to try something new, you will discover it is the most exciting Book you've ever read.

Singing

Singing can lift your spirit as nothing else can. That's right—singing! It's more important than you might think.

How to Nourish the Gift

When troubles get you down, you can sit glumly in your chair, stare at the floor, and feel so sad that you don't know what to do. Or you can get up, start dusting things, and sing a happy tune in spite of your problems, and you'll feel the glow of joy coming back to your heart.

Christian songs are a tonic for the weary soul. They may waken memories of worship services in which God spoke to you in a special way. They may thrill you with a fresh impulse of God's love. Or they may put you in a mood of peaceful reflection on how He has blessed your life.

An insurance salesman was riding the elevated train home from his Chicago office in May of 1915 when he opened his newspaper and learned that a German U-boat had sunk the *Lusitania*. The news threw a pall over the other passengers in his car; they knew that America would now enter the war. A gloomy silence fell upon the group.

Then they passed a street corner where a Salvation Army band was playing gospel songs. The band's melody filled the railroad car, and the people began to hum along:

> We shall sing on that beautiful shore
> The melodious songs of the blest;
> And our spirits shall sorrow no more—
> Not a sigh for the blessing of rest.
>
> In the sweet by and by,
> We shall meet on that beautiful shore;
> In the sweet by and by,
> We shall meet on that beautiful shore.

Their faces brightened. They folded up their newspapers. Even after the sounds of the band died away, the passengers hummed and sang the tune under their breath. It lifted them from hopelessness to heaven.

When your spirit is low and you feel your joy is gone, it's time to sing. You are sure to conquer discouragement when you're "making melody in your heart" (Eph. 5:19).

Laughter

An old proverb says, "Never pick a fight with a laughing man." A person who's laughing is relaxed, exhuberant, and strong.

Laughter is good for the body, but it is even better for the soul. It lets you lay down the burden of worry for a moment to enjoy the humor of your circumstances. It is said that Thomas Edison spent the first half hour of every day in his laboratory reading jokes. His assistants would bring him anecdotes from newspapers and magazines. After he had a good laugh, he felt ready to tackle the problems in his workshop. He was refreshed and invigorated.

I enjoy humorous stories, and I often use humor in my preaching. Jesus did. Read His parables and you will see that He had a keen eye for paradox and whimsy. He said a hypocrite was the sort of person who would strain a gnat out of his soup and then swallow a camel (Matt. 23:24). Or the hypocrite would be oh-so-careful to polish the outside of his bowl and forget to wipe out the moldy leftovers inside (Matt. 23:25). The joke was on the Pharisees. I imagine Jesus' followers threw back their heads and howled.

How to Nourish the Gift

Enjoy the funny situations of life—the zany, ironic turnabouts of life—because Jesus certainly enjoys them. Laugh along with Him, and you'll keep ecstasy in your heart.

Renew Your Strength

Everything you do to nourish the gift of ecstasy will strengthen you as a Christian. Your feelings are a good barometer of your relationship with God, so your ecstasy is simply the *result* of what's happening deep inside. If you're not sure whether you're growing in Christ, take another look at your feelings. If you're happy, confident, and excited about serving the Lord, you can be sure that you are on the right track.

Isaiah realized that our faith and our feelings are linked in a cause-and-effect relationship. He wrote:

> They that wait upon the Lord shall renew their strength; they shall mount up with wings as eagles; they shall run, and not be weary; and they shall walk, and not faint (Isa. 40:31).

As we examine this verse, the cause-and-effect relationship emerges in all its beauty:

"They that wait upon the Lord"—This is where ecstasy begins. When a person yields his life to the Lord and commits himself to serving the Lord completely, he enters the happy family of the King. "They that wait upon the Lord" have the most thrilling and challenging mission of anyone on earth; how can they help but be happy?

57

"Shall renew their strength"—The Lord enables His followers to do everything He sends them to do. He gives them fresh strength to face every obstacle that arises. He rejuvenates them when they get tired.

"They shall mount up with wings as eagles"—This dusty old earth won't get them down. They can fly! They can cross the barriers that would spell "Dead End" to purely human efforts.

"They shall run"—Not only do they reach their goals, but they reach them faster.

"And they shall not be weary"—A long-distance runner will lose the race if he quits on the last lap. But those who serve the Lord get their "second wind" when they need it most. It's the wind of the Holy Spirit!

"And they shall walk, and shall not faint"—In the everyday routine, a happy person will out-perform anyone else. The Christian has a source of strength others don't have; it carries him through the drudgeries of every day.

When the Israelites returned from the Babylonian Exile, they found very disheartening prospects in their homeland. Jerusalem was in ruins; the temple had been destroyed; foreigners had staked claims on their tribal properties. They had every reason to complain.

But Nehemiah proclaimed a day of feasting. He said, "Go your way, eat the fat, and drink the sweet, and send portions unto them for whom nothing is prepared . . . neither be ye sorry; for the joy of the Lord is your strength" (Neh. 8:10).

Remember that. It's important to promote the

gift of joy, because joy is in itself a source of strength. It is also a channel that God can use to revive your haggard spirit.

Take Nehemiah's advice. Renew your joy—and renew your strength.

V

Ecstasy and the Conscious Mind

Into the will of Jesus
  deeper and deeper I go,
Praying for grace to follow,
  seeking His way to know;
Bowing in full surrender
  low at His blessed feet,
Bidding Him take, break me and make,
  till I am molded and meet.

—Oswald J. Smith*

"I've made up my mind—don't confuse me with the facts!" All of us probably have felt like saying that at one time or another—sometimes because we have strong feelings about the issue, but often because the facts *are* confusing. Precious and few are the times we see the facts in proper perspective.

To put it another way, the hard-nosed attitude of "just the facts, ma'am," may be all right for TV detectives, but it doesn't give us all the answers in real life. The answers to our problems may lie beyond the cold, hard reasoning of our conscious minds; in fact, the answers to our most serious problems often do. Yet our conscious minds try to piece together solutions, using the facts. So it's vital for us to understand how the conscious mind operates.

Every aspect of modern society attempts to manipulate the mind. We are assaulted by conflicting forces that seek to rob our minds of happiness and joy. A young executive told his sales force, "If you can't shout in a company president's face and make him buy, you might as well leave now. You won't be around long anyway."[1] That's the prevailing attitude.

The mass media—television and radio, newspapers and magazines—seek to capture the human mind for commerce. Media experts claim that they can relax the mind, "pep up" the mind, create desires to buy, and even teach their audiences to love and hate! The human mind has never been under such pressure.

The Information Explosion

Every day we face a barrage of new information. Even though we develop sophisticated machines to organize, store, and retrieve this information, our minds are dizzied by the whirl of it all. Here is how a popular writer described the Pentagon:

> Every few minutes an assembly gong rings to summon many specialists from their desks to hear a personal report from an expert from some remote part of the world. Meantime, the undone paper work mounts on each desk. And each department daily dispatches personnel by jet to remote areas for more data and reports. Such is the speed of this process of the meeting of the jet plane, the oral report, and the typewriter that those

going forth to the ends of the earth often arrive unable to spell the name of the spot to which they have been sent as experts.[2]

If this kind of confusion dominates the Pentagon, where some of the world's most crucial decisions must be made, is it any wonder that the average citizen is confused?

Security for Sale

As if our minds were not confused enough, we then face the hucksters of strange ideologies. Their printing presses spew out tons of propaganda; their disciples knock at our doors; their lawyers lobby for new laws that will help them propagate their ideas. They tell us how to find "inner peace" and "cosmic consciousness." But their real goal is to shake us down and squeeze out all the money they can get. And they attempt to delude our minds in the process.

Our generation is seeking peace of mind. There are millions of men and women who will clutch at any straw that might save them from the chaos of their everyday lives. They run for it; they ask for it; they pay for it.

Some people hope to find peace by escaping from their problems. They join the "jet set." They fly to the mountains of Switzerland to see the beauty of a sunset. They visit the "fun" cities of Paris and Las Vegas. They languish on the beaches of the Pacific and the West Indies. At the game tables of Monte Carlo they hope to forget their troubles.

Some try suicide to escape their sadness. Others withdraw from society. Criminals try to "rip off" the System. Frustrated couples seek divorce.

But all find that they are more miserable than before.

The Inward Quest

Other people try to find peace by doing exactly the opposite. Instead of trying to escape from the confusion, they study it like an amusing toy. They turn to psychology to learn what they should do, and they find many different kinds of advice.

A leading psychiatrist recently noted how people surrender themselves to the therapist's care. He said:

> Patients do not consider the therapist simply as another person, and the relationship is not a casual matter to them. Patients come to physicians with needs they cannot manage by themselves, no matter how mature and self-sufficient they may be about non-medical matters; and persons come for psychotherapeutic or casework help because they can no longer cope effectively.[3]

In a very real sense, psychiatric counseling is often a matter of life or death. Many people turn to psychiatrists as a last resort, when they feel at their wits' ends. This kind of counseling can help— especially if a person goes to a Christian psychiatrist who understands the interrelationship of the human soul, mind, and body. But psychiatrists often do not understand this, and they give their patients guidance that is more confusing than ever.

For example, some psychologists say that anxiety is a sign that one is trying to repress anger or bitterness. So they tell their patients to take pillows and strike one another until feathers fly around the room. Other counselors say, "Curse God with total abandon and this will relax you." This kind of advice is a lie, and people who try it soon discover as much.

Our nation is emotionally sick. We live in an environment where people habitually promise one thing and do something else. They deceive the very counselors they are talking to. They smile and try to hide their feelings. So psychiatry cannot heal these emotional problems for two reasons: (1) It has a limited understanding of the nature of man, and (2) patients often refuse to admit their real problems.

In the effort to probe deeper into the confusion, some turn to the occult, to meditation, or to eccentric philosophy. One of the most popular avenues is transcendental meditation (TM). Although it has faded from the media limelight recently, TM classes are sprouting up in hundreds of communities across our country, and some colleges have added TM studies to their curricula. Every Christian should realize what TM claims to do.

Proponents say it brings distraught minds into a state of bliss, a place of calm self-consciousness through meditation. It is a meditation technique that places utmost value upon what is happening *now*. It claims there is no such thing as sin or a place of punishment after death, in order to calm the TM disciple's fears. Several people who have practiced TM tell me it seemed to give them a temporary relief from life's pressures, but the illusion faded within the next few hours or days.

Americans practice TM because they have a need that their society and even their religion has not fulfilled. They have lost contact with ecstasy. And so they search everywhere for contentment and peace of mind.

The Source of Ecstasy

True happiness—true peace of mind—is not a product of the mind itself. We cannot find God by simply meditating upon Him, for our limited minds are incapable of comprehending Him. Besides, why should we call upon our minds for the answer to our dilemma? Our minds may already be sick, distorted by the very pressures we are trying to overcome.

The answer lies beyond us. Peace of heart and peace of mind come from God, and they are free for the asking. Anyone can have peace if he will simply say, "Lord, I want it." Notice what Jesus said:

> Come to me, all you who labor and are heavy laden, and I will give you rest. Take My yoke upon you and learn from Me . . . and you will find rest for your souls (Matt. 11:28,29).

Are these the words of a stingy Lord? Does it seem as though Jesus is reluctant to give us peace? Of course not! He only requires us to come to Him, to surrender to Him, and to learn from Him.

Hannah Whitall Smith, a Quaker writer who lived nearly a century ago, wrote, "Salvation comes, not because your faith saves you, but because it links you to the Savior who saves; and your believing is really nothing but the link."[4] Yet what an important link it is! Until we are consciously willing to reach out to Christ, we cannot receive the help He has to offer.

I have often meditated on Michelangelo's painting of "Creation," which spreads across the ceiling of the Sistine Chapel in Rome. The artist shows

God in a cloud of glory with His angels, reaching out to the limp body of Adam. Their fingers almost touch. It seems as if a spark of divine energy has just jumped across the gap. The next time you see that painting, study it carefully: Not only is God reaching out to Adam, but Adam is reaching out to God. That's important. God's power comes when we are willing to receive it.

When life's problems weigh us down, it seems logical to try any number of remedies *except* surrendering to God. We're drawn to self-help books, the advice of friends, and even the desperate ideas that our minds hatch when we're backed into a corner. But the answer is surrender to Jesus Christ.

Pat Kenoyer endured more mental and emotional stress than most of us will ever know. She writes:

> My emotional problems come out of a tragic childhood, followed by a teenage marriage and the care of three children. Add physical anemia and thyroid trouble. There were a few years early in my marriage when I doubted I was going to make it. I was depressed, continually fatigued, almost constantly tempted to commit suicide (I tried twice), and given to emotional excesses. Frankly, in that state, life was not worth living. . . .
>
> But there came a day when I met Christ. Faith connected with His power, and ever so gradually I was released from my mental turmoil. I remember times when a dawning would come to me that through Christ I could be . . . delivered from some mental hang-up I'd suffered for years. In Jesus Christ I became free.[5]

You see, God created in each of us a body, a mind, and a soul; and the soul is the most vital component of our makeup. When the soul finds peace, the mind and body find peace. The soul, mind, and body are so integrally related that a problem of the mind or body often signals a problem of the soul; when the soul-problem is solved the other problems usually get solved too.

This testimony from a young Christian is a good example of what I mean:

> As a non-Christian, I tried to quit smoking hundreds of times. I couldn't do it. I was so hooked on cigarettes I felt I would die without them. I reasoned that smoking was my one pleasure in life as I struggled to raise three small children.
>
> Not long after accepting Christ, I could almost hear Him telling me I was ruining the body He had given me. Already I had been ill with pneumonia and pleurisy twice. Under conviction, I prayed, asking God to give me the power to stop smoking. Suddenly, I discovered I could stop! Once I decided to be *obedient*, God did the rest.[6]

Deciding to be obedient—that's how to find peace of mind! When you surrender your heart to Christ's love and surrender your will to His, you'll begin to see life from a clearer perspective. Things that used to bother you will no longer be so important. Problems that made you cower in fear will shrink to nothingness. When you set your sights on serving the Lord, you'll realize that the emotional "mountains" that seemed to stand in the way are really very easy to climb.

I often face this kind of hurdle in my ministry. Common-sense objections seem to crop up every time we find a new opportunity for outreach. Will there be enough money for our work? Where will we get the kind of staff people we need? Do I personally have enough energy to see it through? These questions haunt me sometimes; but then I remember who I'm working for. He has promised me, "The things which are impossible with men are possible with God" (Luke 18:27). He also says, "If you ask anything in My name, I will do it" (John 14:14). That's all the assurance I need.

V. Raymond Edman tells the story of a man who discovered this peace of mind in the rugged hill country of Ecuador. Mr. Edman was a missionary there. He preached wholehearted commitment to Jesus Christ. One of the leaders of his congregation felt God wanted him to enter the ministry, but his wife stood against it. She said she would not let him leave his well-paying job to become a penniless preacher.

One evening the man came to Mr. Edman, a big bundle under one arm and tears trickling down his cheeks. The missionary turned to Mark 10:29,30 and read to him what Jesus had said: "There is no one who has left house or brothers or sisters or father or mother or wife or children or lands, for My sake and the gospel's, who shall not receive a hundredfold now in this time . . . and in the age to come, eternal life."

The man carried his working clothes in that bundle; he had left his job to serve the Lord. In time, he won his wife to the Lord and together they became effective ministers of the Word.[7]

Surrender to God brings peace of mind.

A New Way of Life

But there's more. After we surrender, we must dedicate ourselves to living a pure life in Christ's name. We call this *holiness*. The Bible says, "Pursue peace with all men, and holiness, without which no one will see the Lord" (Heb. 12:14). In other words, if we want to have true fellowship with God we must be cleansed by Him, and not by our own human efforts.

We might say that *holiness is wholeness*. Holiness means committing all of yourself to God and allowing Him to purge out anything that is not fit for His service. A person who joins the Army gives himself totally to a new way of life. He gets a new identification, a new place to live, a new suit of clothes—even a new haircut! He lets his superiors mold him into the most useful soldier he can be. He finds satisfaction—even happiness—in being extended to the fullest of his abilities. And that's exactly how a Christian feels when he gives his all to the Master.

So first we must say, "Lord, I surrender myself to You." But then we must go on to say, "I dedicate myself to live for You." This is a good life, a clean life, a happy life—and that is what we mean by *ecstasy*.

Accepting the Truth

Accepting God's truth brings peace of mind. By "accepting God's truth," I mean accepting what the Bible says about your relationship with God. Today, many "religious" people try to avoid what the Bible says, either by distorting proper interpretations of Scripture or by discrediting Scripture itself. But if you want to find peace and contentment, you should spend your time studying what the Bible says outright, and then live by it.

A profound Christian thinker of the fourteenth century, Thomas a Kempis, did not lose his sense of priorities as he studied. He wrote: "All holy Scriptures should be read in the spirit in which they were written. . . . The authority of the writer should not affect you, whether he be of little or great learning; but let love of the plain truth lead you to read. Ask not, Who said that? but consider what is said."[8] That's still good advice. We should focus our thoughts upon *what* God is trying to tell us, rather than *how* He is telling us.

The prophet Isaiah said, "Thou wilt keep him in perfect peace, whose mind is stayed on thee: because he trusteth in thee" (Isa. 26:3). When a person disciplines his mind and fixes it upon God, striving only to serve and honor Him, God will give that person the ecstasy of "perfect peace." Isaiah learned that centuries ago, and he's sharing the secret through Scripture.

Of course, fixing our minds upon God is not easy. It never has been. A Catholic monk who lived in France in the late 1600s attempted to fix his mind upon God every minute of every day. He worked in the kitchen of his monastery, so he had to look after countless details involved in feeding the other monks. But he kept thinking about God all through the day. He said:

> I worshipped Him the oftenest that I could, keeping my mind in His holy presence, and recalling it as often as I found it wandering from Him. I found no small pain in this exercise, and yet I continued in it . . . not troubling or disquieting myself when my mind had wandered involuntarily. . . . At all times, every hour, every minute, even in the height of my business, I drove away from my mind everything that was capable of interrupting my thought of God.[9]

Despite all the difficulties involved, you will find that your life is more peaceful and happy when you focus your thoughts on God. You will be less likely to get upset when frustrations come your way. You will not fly into a rage when someone offends you. You will be more conscious of God, so you will be more concerned about pleasing Him and responding to His wishes. Your state of mind will be oriented toward pleasing your divine Companion more than your human companions. That's how it ought to be.

The human mind is the world's greatest battlefield. The devil struggles for control of our minds, in hopes of leading us totally away from God. Yet the Lord challenges Satan for control of our minds as He confronts Satan with the truth of His written Word. He gives us the choice of believing the devil's delicious lies or the plain truth of Scripture.

It's not an easy choice to make. But if we choose the truth, we will find more happiness than the devil could ever promise.

VI

Ecstasy and the Subconscious Mind

Peace, perfect peace—
in this dark world of sin?
The blood of Jesus whispers
peace within.

—Edward H. Bickersteth[1]

Half a century ago, British theologian Leslie D. Weatherhead wrote a much-publicized book to explore psychology from a Christian point of view. Although I don't buy Dr. Weatherhead's humanistic ideas, I like the title of his book: *Psychology in Service of the Soul.*

Psychology *ought* to serve us as we seek to cultivate our spiritual lives. It helps us understand our mental and emotional makeup, and it tries to show what makes us "tick" internally. We need to understand these things if we want to be the whole, happy people God intended us to be. Joy must shine from the inside out.

Unfortunately, Satan knows that. So when he wants to destroy our happiness, he often begins working on our inner selves. Psychology can help us understand how he does this, and we can use psychological insights to guard the subconscious mind from his joy-robbing influence.

What Is the Subconscious?

First, we should consider what the subconscious mind is. It covers a much broader scope of activity than the conscious mind. The mind is somewhat like an iceberg: Only a small tip appears above the surface (the conscious mind), while the greatest mass is hidden (the subconscious mind). The subconscious mind contains a wealth of information that the conscious mind has never identified. The subconscious is *subliminal* ("below the threshhold"); it is that vast realm of thinking that lies below the threshhold of consciousness. It includes the mental processes that are always going on at the edge or margin of our conscious awareness. The subconscious is at work every hour of every day.

Through our eyes and our ears, sights and sounds register in our brains as facts. Yet many of the things we see and hear are not immediately perceived by our conscious mind; they are stored in the subconscious. We base our actions upon all the things we have seen or heard, whether we are conscious of these experiences or not.

But how do we know what is in the subconscious? That's not an easy question to answer. The contents of our subconscious storehouse can surface at the most unexpected moments. Yet these times reveal much about what is happening in our subconscious.

For example, the subconscious may emerge while we sleep. Sigmund Freud, C. G. Jung, and other psychologists have concluded that our subconscious minds supply most of our dreams. This often affects how we behave after we awake. Often I dream I am preaching to a large congregation and giving an altar call. I dream I am praising God for the way people responded to the message. I wake up with a flood of joy flowing through me.

A crisis can bring forth facts or ideas that we have stored in the subconscious. Often a student will encounter a test question that stumps him, and he will follow a "hunch" that proves to be correct. Later he finds he had read over the information weeks before the test without paying any particular attention to that specific fact; he had filed it in his subconscious, and the test brought it out.

Hypnosis can reveal what is in the subconscious, and some therapists use this technique to unravel their patients' problems. (But it is also a dangerous method, because the therapist can use hypnosis to tinker with his patient's subconscious mind, causing more problems.)

The Power of Suggestion

The more we learn about the subsconscious mind, the more we realize that it plays a vital role in our decision-making. It is the storehouse of memory and the center of moral values. It guides our conscious minds in the choices we make every day. So if someone else gains control of our subconscious, he has virtually gained control of our lives. Psychologist George W. Crane says:

> From the standpoint of psychology . . . subconscious or marginal learning has today come to be regarded as of even more significance than was frequently thought. The psychoanalysts work with the habits

75

which have been acquired unwittingly by their patients and the advertisers depend for much of their success upon the subconscious or marginal learning of their public.[2]

Psychologists have discovered the amazing and frightening form of communication that Crane alludes to. The average person may not be aware of it, but the communications media and advertisers use it very skillfully. It's technically called *subliminal suggestion*. Here is how it works: The advertiser or other communicator gives his audience an important message, one that grabs their attention. But at the same time he gives them this direct bit of communication, he gives them a subtle, indirect message that their subconscious minds will pick up.

For example, a few years ago some theaters began using subliminal suggestions to sell refreshments. During the intermission between movies, the projectionist would show a series of important announcements about fire exits and rules against smoking in the theater. At the same time, he would flash pictures of food on the screen—hot dogs, popcorn, cold drinks, and so on—showing each for just a fraction of a second. It was too quick to register in the audience's conscious minds, but their subconscious minds realized it and their mouths began to water. So they slipped out to the theater's snack bar.

Certain department stores have used subliminal suggestion by playing mood music for their shoppers. Spritely, happy tunes put people in a mood to forget their budget problems and buy more items than they otherwise would. Some stores have even played ad messages behind the music. Shoppers did not *consciously* notice this, but they began buying the items that the store needed to "move."

Our courts have outlawed these more devious kinds of commercial suggestion. But advertisers still use other forms of subliminal suggestion. Have you ever wondered why cigarette ads show smokers in beautiful country scenes? Or why beer and liquor ads show happy, youthful people having fun? It's because they're giving us subconscious messages; they're trying to convince our inner minds that smoking refreshes us and that drinking is enjoyable. In this way, they create a mood that triggers a decision to buy.

The Secretary-General of the United Nations has concluded that it is now technically possible for satellites orbiting the earth to transmit messages directly to home television sets everywhere in the world. Foreign governments could send us subliminal messages behind our favorite TV programs, and we wouldn't know it. The United Nations staff warns that communications of this type could brainwash millions of people over several months or years.

When news reporters tell the facts of a war, they convey their feelings as well. Newscasters may seem to portray national leaders in an objective way, but if you listen closely you will detect words that betray the reporter's biases. Does he say the president "declared" something, or that he "claimed" it? Does he say a union leader "rejected" accusations against him or that he "denied" them? We are bombarded by thousands of these words every day, and they can gradually shape what we think about the world around us.

Religious leaders use subliminal suggestion too, and some have led sincere Christians into heresy by this method. It's a problem that has threatened the church since the first century. Jude, the brother of James, warned his Christian friends that "certain men have crept in unnoticed, . . . ungodly men, who turn the grace of our God into licentiousness and deny the only Lord God and our Lord Jesus Christ" (Jude 4). Today we see hundreds of evangelists and pastors who profess to be loyal Christians, but who lure people into accepting all sorts of crazy, blasphemous ideas.

Guarding the Subconscious

So what we do with the subconscious mind is very serious business. As the end of time approaches, we must realize that it is a matter of spiritual life or death. John says, "Even now many antichrists have come, by which we know it is the last hour. . . . He is antichrist who denies the Father and the Son" (1 John 2:18,22). "For many deceivers have gone out into the world who do not confess Jesus Christ as coming in the flesh. This is a deceiver and an antichrist" (2 John 7).

Some religious leaders say openly that Jesus is not the Son of God. But many, many more *suggest* it by what they say and do, denying the power of Christ, the judgment of God, and even the truthfulness of Scripture. Thus they train their followers to believe a lie.

A Christian must guard his subconscious mind as carefully as he guards his conscious mind. He must protect the very center and core of his decision-making powers. The apostle Peter said, "Gird up

78

the loins of your mind" (1 Pet. 1:13). That's certainly good advice. We should strengthen our minds against every influence—both obvious and subtle—that would turn us away from God. There are some very practical ways to do this:

DON'T read pornographic literature. When you read filth, your mind accumulates filth. It is simply impossible to read about lust, promiscuity, and perversion and keep your mind focused upon the Lord.

DON'T listen to "hard rock" music. America is inundated by music that attempts to shatter all sense of joy, music filled with cursing and blasphemy. When you listen to this music, its perverse values seep into your mind.

DON'T interfere with the normal functions of the mind. You should never tamper with your mind by abusing drugs or alcohol. You should not experiment with hypnosis, ESP, or spiritism in an effort to bypass the mind's logical functions.

Enough for the negatives. Now let us consider some positive things that help to strengthen the mind:

DO read the Word of God. The psalmist said, "Thy word have I hid in mine heart, that I might not sin against thee" (Ps. 119:11). When we treasure God's Word deep within us, it will keep us on the path of obedience.

DO converse with God through prayer. Invite Him to examine and correct your innermost thoughts. Then heed what He says.

DO bear witness to what the Lord is doing in your life. Each time you share your story, you will depend upon Him to tell you what to say. This makes you more sensitive to His direction.

Consecrated to God

God will keep our minds pure if we allow Him to. God made each of us a free moral agent; we can live and think as we please. A sinful person chooses to ignore God and satisfy his own desires. All of us inherit this tendency. But when we repent of our sins, our minds are changed. We stop putting ourselves first and begin putting God first. God cleanses our conscious and subconscious minds, but He still expects us to be their custodians. And if we expose our minds to ungodly influences, they will be corrupted again—consciously, subconsciously, or both. Every temptation from the devil is first presented to the mind. It is our first line of spiritual defense.

God wants to bring His joy into our subconscious minds. All we have to do is yield ourselves to Him. Paul told the Christians at Rome, "Do not be conformed to this world, but be transformed by the renewing of your mind." When God renews someone's mind, that individual's life will exhibit "that good and acceptable and perfect will of God" (Rom. 12:2).

The subconscious mind becomes a treasury of joyful memories, a place where God's daily graces are pondered. Like the mainspring of a clock, it feels every turn of God's leading and brings it back to our consciousness when we get discouraged or confused. It points us toward decisions that will honor God when the conscious mind cannot decide what to do.

The subconscious mind will be attuned to God because it has stored experiences of God's love day after day.

Like a Computer

As I mentioned before, this happens only when the conscious mind keeps a vigilant guard over what the subconscious is exposed to. We might say the subconscious is like a computer; it can feed back only what has been put into it. If you feed false information into a computer or if you tell it to process information in an illogical way, it will give you erroneous answers. The subconscious is like that: Expose it to ungodly ideas and it will begin to give you ungodly impulses.

You may think it strange to compare the human mind to a computer, but psychologists see many parallels between the two. In fact, psychologists are now studying computer research in order to find clues to solving mental and emotional problems.[3] They are especially interested in *cybernetics*. This discipline considers, among other things, what sort of information is fed into computers and how they are told to evaluate the information. As we have already seen, our subconscious minds are constantly evaluating the information our conscious minds receive; in fact, the subconscious can override the logic of the conscious mind when it's time to respond to that information.

Cybernetics reveals that *the way information is handled affects the outcome just as much as the information itself.* So a carnal subconscious mind will interpret the facts of the world in a carnal fashion, even though it sees evidence of God's activity. Francis Schaeffer explains it this way:

> The tragedy of our situation today is that men and women are being fundamentally affected by the new way of looking at truth and yet they have never analyzed the drift which has taken place. Young people from Christian homes are brought up in the old framework of truth. Then they are subjected to the modern framework. In time they become confused because they do not understand the alternatives with which they are presented. Confusion becomes bewilderment, and before long they are overwhelmed.[4]

Our minds are trained to interpret the world in a certain way—call it a "framework," a "mindset," or whatever. The carnal subconscious mind can ignore God's love in the happenings of each day, while the Christian subconscious mind can discern Him in the midst of tragedy. This difference of outlook affects everything we do.

Several years ago, a plastic surgeon named Maxwell Malz discovered that many of his patients were unhappy with the results of his work. They expected that their lives would be happier if they got a facelift, had a nose straightened, or had some other cosmetic problem corrected.

But they came back to Dr. Malz's office discouraged, dejected, even angry. Some said, "Of course, the bump is no longer on my nose—but my nose still *looks* the same." Or, "I look just the same as before—you didn't do a thing."

After studying hundreds of cases, Dr. Malz found that the "failures" were people who viewed themselves and the world around them *as if* they were still disfigured. He concluded that the secret of full recovery was for the patient to change his opinion of himself.

He found that this applies to other areas of life as well. One day a businessman told him, "How can I possibly be happy? I've just lost $200,000 on the stock market. I am ruined and disgraced."

"You can be happier by not adding your own opinion to the facts," Dr. Malz replied. "It is a fact that you lost $200,000. It is your opinion that you are ruined and disgraced."[5]

The conscious mind organizes facts, but the subconscious shapes opinions, and these opinions affect how the conscious mind does its work.

Surrendered to the Spirit

The subconscious is also the seat of desire. When surrendered to God, it will bring forth godly desires; when it is not, it will bring forth selfish desires. So a person who has not fully surrendered himself to the Lord may find his (holy) conscious mind struggling against his (unholy) subconscious mind. This frustrating situation must be resolved.

Many psychologists say the conscious mind must subdue the subconscious. Others say the conscious must open better channels of communication with the subconscious and try to hear what it is really saying.

But there's a better solution: Surrender both the conscious and the subconscious mind to the Holy Spirit. "For those who live according to the flesh set their minds on the things of the flesh, but those who live according to the Spirit, the things of the Spirit. For to be carnally minded is death, but to be spiritually minded is life and peace" (Rom. 8:5,6). Mark that: A person who is "spiritually minded"—one who has surrendered his whole mind to the Spirit—finds life and *peace*. He has no more struggles between the opposing forces of his mind. Instead, he is relaxed, confident, and happy. He is at peace.

Tim LaHaye, a well-known Christian psychologist, has observed this in the lives of people he has counseled:

> A singing, thanks-giving heart and a submissive spirit, independent of circumstances, are so unnatural that they can only be ours through the filling of the Holy Spirit. The Spirit of God is able to change the gloomy or griping heart into a song-filled, thankful heart. He is also able to solve man's natural rebellion problem by increasing his faith to the point that he really believes the best way to live is in submission to the will of God.[6]

Each person must make a conscious decision to yield his life to the Holy Spirit. In this sense, the conscious mind controls what the subconscious is able to do. Unless you ask for the Holy Spirit's infilling, your subconscious mind will remain oriented to the world's ideals. It will evaluate with selfish motives everything you see and hear. No matter how many church services you attend or how many Bible verses you memorize, a carnal subconscious mind will continue to ask: "What's in it for me?" or "How can I use this to gain prestige?" It will be constantly dissatisfied. But when you allow the Spirit to take full control of your life, your entire being—mind, body, and soul—will turn God-ward. Then your mind must keep you oriented that way.

If you let your mind wander away from God and

fix itself upon selfish desires once again, be prepared for trouble. The world's ungodly standards will begin to infiltrate your subconscious, and before long you will find yourself "instinctively" disobeying God. At times like this, your conscious mind must act as a spiritual policeman; it must overrule the subconscious in favor of what you consciously know is right. The Holy Spirit will enable you to do this.

An Episcopal minister named Samuel M. Shoemaker knew this kind of struggle until he yielded himself entirely to the Holy Spirit's leadership. Later he said, "The difficult thing about guidance is not the receiving or recognizing of it: It is the truly wanting it, so that we come to God stripped, honest, and without pretense. Then He can speak directly."[7]

Our minds do not have to be in turmoil; God is always ready to give us peace when we submit our minds to Him.

Joy From the Inside Out

When does an apple begin? Not with a blossom; that's just a fanfare to the final act. Not with the twig; that's just the supporting cast of this drama. Not even with the roots of the tree; true, they are the advance crew for the whole company, but they are not the beginning. No, an apple begins with a *seed*. From the seed all the foliage of the tree springs forth; and finally the fruit comes, bearing more seed within it. The beginning, the end, and all that an apple is—you can find *inside* the apple.

It's the same way with ecstasy. It begins *inside* a person, when he asks Jesus Christ to be his Lord.

And as long as a person's life radiates this kind of joy, you can be sure it's coming from deep inside, where Christ is on the throne. A person can try to mimic the ecstasy of his Christian friends, and he can even fool himself into thinking he has been able to master it. But unless he has the seed of ecstasy planted in his innermost self, his act will soon be over.

True joy starts on the inside and comes out. It's the result of something Christ has done at the very core of someone's personality, even in the subconscious mind. He has inspired that person to *repent* (literally, to "change his mind"). All the changes others may see outwardly are just the fruit of that basic inward change.

If you want ecstasy, you need to let Christ have the seedbed of your life. You need to let Him have your mind—*all* of it.

VII
Imitation Ecstasy

No matter how helpful a faith is, if it is not true, we want nothing of it. We would rather go to pieces on the basis of honesty than to patch up a civilization on the basis of fiction or wishful thinking.

—D. Elton Trueblood[1]

Imitation is the most sincere form of flattery, or so it is said. Not long after McDonald's introduced the "Quarter-Pounder," every hamburger stand in town was selling quarter-pound burgers. Polaroid unveiled a camera that "hands you the picture," and the next year its competitors' cameras were cranking out pictures, too. And remember the Teflon craze? It seemed as though every frying pan in America was going to be coated with the brown, non-stick plastic.

Sociologists call it the "bandwagon effect." Americans have learned that it is easier to imitate someone else—to hop on their "bandwagon"—than it is to play their own tune.

Today many people are trying to imitate the ecstasy of the Christian life. They want the dividends without investing themselves. Greedy men and women are hatching far-out philosophies to offer the public a "new and improved" version of what Jesus taught. Some of them use Satanism and witchcraft to attract people who are interested in the supernatural. Others sell illegal drugs to offer their friends an easy "high." These imitators of ecstasy are making extravagant claims for the false happiness they are peddling. So we should take a moment to consider *what is not ecstasy*, so we don't get suckered into their schemes.

Acid Tests

How can we tell the difference between true ecstasy and contrived, artificial ecstasy? It isn't easy when the imitators seem so appealing.

A gold prospector in the Old West would carry a vial of acid to test the nuggets he found. He knew the acid would dissolve iron pyrite, the attractive-looking "fool's gold," but it wouldn't dissolve real gold nuggets. So when he was in doubt, he could use a few drops of acid to test the ore.

You can use God's Word in the same way. When you encounter an idea or lifestyle that promises to bring ecstasy and you're not sure whether it's the real thing, give it these acid tests from Scripture.

• *Ecstasy means peace.* "Great peace have they which love thy law: and nothing shall offend them" (Ps. 119:165). And what about those who live outside of God's ecstasy? "The way of peace they know not ... they have made them crooked paths: whosoever goeth therein shall not know peace" (Isa. 59:8).

Before I was born again in Christ, I was a troubled person. I was afraid to die and afraid to live. I was

88

afraid my parents would find out what a scoundrel I was, and afraid my friends *wouldn't* find out! My face betrayed a life of sadness and depression. But when Jesus came into my heart, I received an ecstatic peace that words cannot describe. A troubled person became untroubled.

If pursuing some kind of so-called ecstasy fills you with anxiety, tension, or fear, it's not real ecstasy. I know that from God's Word and from my own experience.

• *Ecstasy means renewal.* It does not use you up; it fills you up. "Therefore we do not lose heart. But though our outward man is perishing, yet the inward man is being renewed day by day" (2 Cor. 4:16). Sitting quietly and reading the Bible can move your inner being gracefully toward renewal, if you yield yourself to the Lord.

Some promoters of false ecstasy try to sell you a routine of some trifling little exercise, which they say will "expand your consciousness" or "lift you to a higher plane." But all they really achieve is boredom and weariness. Treat that kind of "ecstasy" for what it is—a counterfeit!

• *Ecstasy means Christ.* If some "sure-fire" method for finding happiness does not glorify the Lord Jesus Christ, look out! It's a fake. Paul told the Christians at Colossae, "Whatever you do, do it heartily, as to the Lord and not to men, knowing that from the Lord you will receive the reward of the inheritance; for you serve the Lord Christ" (Col. 3:23,24). If you cannot do something "heartily, as to the Lord," then you cannot expect it to give you ecstasy.

The console of a great pipe organ has several rows of buttons and sliding tabs called "stops." Each "stop" controls the amount of air that can flow through a certain set of pipes. Before playing a piece of music, the organist sets the stops to get the desired tone and balance.

We might say that the life of ecstasy "pulls out all the stops"; it holds back nothing from the Lord. An ecstatic Christian throws himself wholeheartedly into everything, because he does everything for the Lord. The moment he begins to do some things that are *not* Christ-honoring, using the excuse that some of these things are fun, he sets a "stop" on his life. The music of his soul loses its zest. The ecstasy begins to fade.

The Imitators

These acid tests from Scripture can help us distinguish the true way of happiness from all the imitators that rival it. Let's apply these tests to some of the things that are said to bring happiness:

• *Health*. I have heard many hospital patients say, "If only I could get well again, I would be happy!" That makes sense, especially when you consider that our society treats sick people like outcasts. We expect everyone to strive toward the ideal of physical fitness. If you're not jogging, bicycling, dieting, playing in sports, or cheering those who are, you're an oddball. And if you *can't* do these things, you are of all Americans most miserable. Or so it seems. Even TV commercials observe that "when you've got your health, you've got just about everything."

But that's not necessarily so. Every year hundreds of people with normal, healthy bodies commit suicide. On the other hand, some of the happiest people I've ever known were sick and crippled.

In an earlier chapter I mentioned Joni Eareckson, who surrendered her life to Christ after she was paralyzed by a swimming accident. By the standards of our society, Joni should be miserable and bitter. She has lost the use of her arms and legs, and she needs a mechanical respirator to aid her breathing. She will be confined to a wheelchair for the rest of her life.

But she is happy! Christ has filled her heart with a determined desire to live a useful life. She learned to draw by holding a felt-tipped pen between her teeth, and her beautiful illustrations now appear on stationery, greeting cards, and framed prints.

Joni is happier than most "normal" people, and I could name dozens of other handicapped people who have just as much enthusiasm for life. If health is the way to happiness, how can we explain the Joni Earecksons of this world?

Now apply the acid tests to the claim that health brings ecstasy.

Does health mean peace of mind? Not always. Does it give you renewal? In some ways, but not in every way. Does it draw you closer to Christ? Perhaps, but that is not its primary goal.

Health is certainly important. God made our bodies, and we should use them to honor Him. But health cannot give the deep, eternal joy that every person longs for.

• *Wealth.* Many people have struggled with financial problems for so long that they believe wealth would make them happy. "If I had all the money I need," such a person says, "I could take life easy. I could have time to enjoy my family. I could forget all the worries that bother me now." Granted, wealth can be a great blessing and many wealthy people have found happiness. J. C. Penney founded a chain of department stores that made him fabulously wealthy as he practiced the Golden Rule. People who knew him testify that he was a happy man. R. G. LeTourneau made millions from the sale of heavy-duty construction equipment, and his life bubbled over with joy. We could mention hundreds of others.

But all would agree that wealth itself does not bring happiness. The pursuit of wealth can destroy you. Even after you acquire wealth, you may find that it gives you boredom and restlessness. If you do not have the Source of happiness on the inside, wealth cannot give you happiness on the outside.

Wealth does not automatically give a person peace of mind. If it did, why would rich people need psychoanalysts? It does not bring renewal, because it usually carries burdens of responsibility that weigh a person down. And it is not always Christ-centered. Mr. Penney and dozens of other Christian millionaires accepted Christ *before* they made their fortune, but very few have been converted after they became rich.

Wealth is very fragile. Fortunes are made and lost every day, and while a person can say, "Easy come, easy go," it's not easy to accept the sudden loss of wealth. Money and property can exact a heavy toll in personal strength and sensitivity, and they certainly do not insure that a person will have a joyful life.

• *Rest.* When some people think of happiness, they imagine a tropical island where they will never need to work, a place where pleasant breezes always blow and beautiful native girls bring them pineapples and coconuts. Or they imagine themselves in retirement, with no more time clocks to punch or children to dress for school. In other words, they think inactivity would bring them happiness.

But again, experience proves this wrong. I have spent many months in Florida, where many retired couples while away the hours in drowsy quietness. They are not happy. They feel restless and dissatisfied without something to do. On the other hand, I work long hours every day and I am always happy. I find that people working on useful projects are the most excited, enthusiastic, and ebullient people I meet all day.

So even though rest is beneficial, it is not the essence of happiness. Rest is an *effect* of ecstasy, not its source.

• *Illegitimate Sex.* The massage parlors, pornographic theaters, and prostitution rings promise their customers fulfillment and delight. Instead, they give disillusionment, guilt, regret, and even disease. Illicit sex produces frustration. It causes confusion. It gives Satan a brief opportunity to control a person's desires. This does not fit the character of ecstasy.

God created human sexuality as a beautiful expression of the harmony of His creation. He reserved it for marriage, to bless and benefit a man and woman who commit their lives to one another. Promiscuous sex is a grotesque distortion of God's plan. By no means does it bring happiness to those who indulge in it.

Apply the acid tests to illegitimate sex, and you will see the shallowness of this fabled source of ecstasy. Does it bring peace of mind? Ask the young couple who have sacrificed their morals in the passion of a "heavy date." Does it bring renewal? Ask the prostitutes who plod the streets of our cities, selling their bodies for a living. Does it bring a person to Christ? Ask the thousands of men and women whose lives have been wrecked by adultery and promiscuity. If they admit the truth, they will confess that illicit sex has not made them happy.

● *Drugs and Alcohol.* At the end of the 1960s, millions of young people began experimenting with drugs. They hoped to find an escape from the pressures of war, political trouble, and competition for jobs. Drugs gave them a temporary "high." They propelled their minds into an unreal world of hallucination and twisted logic. But in some cases, minds were not able to return to reality; they were devastated by the chemicals that were supposed to bring deliverance. One by one, drug users discovered that they were "high" for a moment but degraded for the rest of their lives.

Soon young people turned to alcohol as a more convenient, more predictable route of escape. We are witnessing the greatest epidemic of teen-age alcoholism that our country has ever known, and it is fired by this thirst for escape and peace. But the young alcoholics of the 1970s are beginning to realize that alcohol is a false form of ecstasy, too. The thrill ends when you reach the bottom of the glass.

Alcohol can create the illusion of joy, but it cannot create the reality. It makes the drinker think he is rich when he is poor, that things are all right when they are all wrong. The pleasant mood of social drinking is an advertised lie; although alcohol offers you ecstasy, it cannot deliver the goods.

● *Political Freedom*. While many people search for ecstasy through physical freedom or mental freedom, others try the avenue of political freedom. They believe that if they gain freedom from persecution, they will have all they need to be happy. And they can quote many eminent philosophers to support the idea.

Freedom is certainly a precious thing. Nearly every week, our newspapers tell of families that escape from Communist countries, leaving their relatives and all their possessions behind. Russian dancers, artists, and scientists risk their lives by defecting to the West. They know only too well the importance of having freedom.

But political freedom does not guarantee happiness, or all Americans would be happy. And the lack of freedom does not keep a person from happiness. Jesus was happy, though persecuted. He was arrested for no good reason. He was sentenced to die. Yet He stood tall and strong above every persecution and personal obstacle. He was confident and happy despite the fact that He lost His "civil rights." So we cannot equate political freedom with ecstasy; it is an appealing imitation, but an imitation nonetheless.

● *"Meditation" and "Expanded Consciousness."* Several modern cults promise to lead a person to ecstasy through "transcendental meditation," "expanded consciousness," and the like. Each has a different method, but they all have the same goal: to provide relief from tension through mental detachment. They teach people to empty their minds of everything and concentrate on something outside themselves—perhaps a philosophical idea, a beautiful object, or even a nonsense word. The purpose is to dispel all normal thoughts from your mind and allow inner relaxation.

Although these cults promise eternal bliss, their disciples come and go. They experiment with the cults, become disenchanted, and go elsewhere. Ironically, many of these meditation cults come from India, one of the saddest spots on the face of the earth. Apparently the gurus and yogis failed to bring peace to their own countrymen, so they tried to plant their ideas on foreign soil. But even here they have failed to bear much fruit.

Once again, let us submit them to the acid tests of ecstasy. Do the cults bring peace of mind? Only if you call mindlessness "peace of mind." Do they bring renewal? Not really. They lead their disciples into confusion, frustration, and sometimes despair. They instruct their disciples to let down their mental defenses to random eccentric thoughts, which opens the way for alien spirits to enter. These alien, demonic spirits can lead a person into deep depression before he realizes what is happening.

From the beginning of time, human beings have tried to expand their consciousness. In fact, in the Garden of Eden, Eve tried to expand her mind to become like God! But as a result, she fell away from God. Every way of acquiring wisdom that excludes God's way is doomed to fail.

• *Witchcraft.* Not many people openly profess to practice witchcraft, but it has a strong attraction for curious minds. Witchcraft, the occult, spiritualism, and astrology are all cut from the same bolt of cloth. They all attempt to peer into some "secret" source of wisdom that will give a person special insights or special powers for coping with his problems. Their practices range all the way from wearing "good-luck charms" like rabbits' feet to communicating with the dead through seances and Ouija boards. They all boil down to the same thing—an effort to bypass God in supernatural matters.

Witchcraft or any of its kindred practices will bring a person under the judgment of God. Witchcraft stands on the foundation of fear, superstition, and hatred. It invokes demonic powers to accomplish its ends. So it undermines the very basis of a person's fellowship with God. Although it promises the ecstasy of superior knowledge or power, it brings only the tragedy of a godless life.

True Ecstasy

Ecstasy is so widely imitated because it is so earnestly desired. But why peg your hopes on the imitations of ecstasy when you can have the genuine experience? Many people live in ecstasy *without* any of the things we have listed above. They are happy in spite of illness, persecution, poverty, and personal failure. You see, they have learned that ecstasy comes not from any *thing*, but from a Person.

My ecstasy began with my new birth, when I accepted Jesus Christ as my Savior and Lord. It did not come by sitting down cross-legged and throwing my mind into neutral. It came when I said, "O God, I am sorry for my sins. Forgive me and come into my heart." At that moment I was spiritually reborn. Jesus Christ cleansed me of every ungodly thought and deed, and He filled me with His wonderful peace. My life of sadness and depression was gone. Nothing else could have wrought that kind of change in my life. I know because I tried plenty of imitations before I found true ecstasy.

Charles W. Colson, President Nixon's political "hatchet man," climbed several rungs on the prestige ladder at the White House before he realized that it left him more hapless and discouraged than ever before. On a long, thoughtful vacation in Maine he surrendered his life to Christ. Sitting beside the Atlantic surf, Colson offered a simple prayer of repentance and faith in the Lord Jesus Christ. Notice how he describes that experience:

> With these few words that morning . . . came a sureness of mind that matched the depth of feeling in my heart. There came something more: strength and serenity, a wonderful new assurance about life, a fresh perception of myself and the world around me. In the process, I felt old fears, tensions, and animosities draining away. I was coming alive to things I'd never seen before; as if God was filling the barren void . . . filling it to its brim with a new kind of awareness.[2]

Underline that phrase, "the barren void." It describes what Charles Colson and thousands of other people have found as they built up their political power and prestige. This way of life seems full of excitement and emotional rewards, but those who have been there find that politics is not enough to satisfy. If you depend on it for the ecstasy of life, you will be painfully disappointed. Like all the other imitations of ecstasy, political power by itself is a "barren void."

But Charles Colson went on to find the Source of real ecstasy. Read again how he describes his feelings when he yielded his life to Christ. He says he received *"strength* and *serenity,* a wonderful new *assurance* about life, a *fresh perception* of myself and the world around me." That's a good description of ecstasy, isn't it? And when we apply the acid tests of Scripture to Mr. Colson's experience, it proves to be genuine.

A person who has found real ecstasy can look up to the heavens and say, "I thank You, O God, who created the heavens and the earth and all that is in them. I am glad that I know You now. I am sure that I am Yours and You are mine, that I am a child of God beyond any doubt. My spirit bears witness with Yours and tells me that I am Your child."

All the false ecstasies of the world come to us with the same proposition: "Just buy me and you will have peace and joy." This simply is not true. Only God can offer us real ecstasy through His Son, Jesus Christ. There is "joy unspeakable and full of glory" for those who put their trust in Him (1 Pet. 1:8).

Many people are groaning to God about their situations in life. They are living life in the minor key, telling themselves and everyone around them that they would be happy "if only . . ." They had better wake up to the fact that God made each of us to live a life of joy—great joy, wonderful joy! Every person can have a life of ecstasy; everyone can live in the major key.

Ecstasy is not something that drags us back and drags us down, throwing a cloud of discouragement over our heads. It does not give us an attitude of resignation that says, "Oh, well, this is the best I can hope for." That's not the kind of ecstasy I am talking about.

I am talking about life that has the prospect of a clear, blue sky. I am talking about spending every day in the warm rays of the Sun of Righteousness (Mal. 4:2). I am talking about having a heart so full of joy that it overflows in smiles, laughter, and words of encouragement day after day. That's real ecstasy.

And all the imitators of ecstasy cannot hold a candle to the genuine experience.

VIII

The God of Ecstasy

In the Bible . . . we have set before us a conception of God that is more profound, more exalted, more awe-inspiring, more gladdening, and heart-thrilling and ennobling, than is to be found in any or in all of the profoundest philosophies of the past or even of the present day. . . .

—R. A. Torrey[1]

When I was only twenty years old I became a missionary. Since that time, I have visited over one hundred nations of the world. I have visited the temples of Tibet; in fact, I have slept on a cot beneath a twenty-foot-high image of Buddha inside one of those temples. I have seen paintings and statues representing hundreds of Hindu gods—angry gods, gods of vengeance, and ugly, unmerciful gods.

We do not serve such a god. We serve the true God of ecstasy and joy. We live by the joy we receive from God. We can face every tomorrow with the strength of His joy (Neh. 8:10).

I have shared this with thousands of people in my travels around the globe. They often ask me, "How do you know there is a God of ecstasy? How do you know the nature of a God you have never seen? How can you, with your finite abilities, pretend to understand the Infinite?"

This is a difficult assignment, to say the least. If we had to rely solely upon our senses and our minds' logical processes, we would not be able to fathom the nature of God. But we have three sources of revealed knowledge that tell us He is a God of ecstasy.

The first of these is *the Bible*. This Book reveals God's majesty and glory, it describes His temperament, and it explains many things we would like to know about Him. The Bible contains more than 20,000 references to God. The first verse, the last verse, and all the narrative in between speak of God's dealings with man. It is truly a remarkable Book.

The second source of revealed knowledge is *our experience*. God did not end His interaction with man when John wrote the last line of Revelation. He continues to teach us and guide us through the problems and challenges we face every day.

The third source of revealed knowledge is *the inward witness of the Holy Spirit*. Jesus promised that "when He, the Spirit of truth, has come, He will guide you into all truth ... and He will tell you things to come" (John 16:13). This promise was fulfilled on the day of Pentecost, when the Holy Spirit came upon Jesus' followers and gave them power to bear witness to Him. The Holy Spirit is still with us, and He reveals things about God that we cannot perceive from Scripture or from our own experiences.

So, God has not cut off His communications with us. He reveals Himself to us in spite of our limited ability to understand. He tells us loud and clear that He is full of ecstasy, and He wants to share that ecstasy with us.

He Creates

The Book of Genesis opens with these words: "In the beginning God created the heaven and the earth." The very first page of the Bible shows us that God is a Creator, not a destroyer. He is not intent on shattering our hopes and dreams. He creates; He produces; He fulfills; He provides everything in this world that we enjoy. James says, "Every good gift and every perfect gift is from above, and comes down from the Father of lights, with whom there is no variation or shadow of turning" (James 1:17). In other words, God gives us every pleasure of life. He made the entire world with all of its beauties, and He allows us to have the privilege of enjoying it.

Mort Crim is a newscaster who has covered some of the most historic events of our time. He recently commented on what it means to know that God created us.

> If life is no more than a cosmic accident, a mindless joke, a swirl of confusion and color splashed across the black backdrop of meaningless time, then perhaps the discotheque is man's truest expression of reality. . . . There, in miniature, is the story and the glory of life.
>
> If, however, life is the considered output of love and intellect; if human existence is the product of purpose; if life is more than something to do while waiting to die; then the truest expression of reality is man living purposefully.[2]

Indeed, this world *is* a "product of purpose." God made the earth and everything on it—including you and me—because He had a wonderful purpose in mind. He is not offended by our bodies or our handiwork or anything else that is in all of creation, because it is all *His* creation. He enjoys it. He wants us to enjoy it with Him. And He wants us to carry out the purpose He gave every person: to serve and honor Him.

God created you to be a healthy, happy person. He gave you wholesome desires. As Pastor J. Wallace Hamilton once said, "There are no bad instincts, just as there are no bad notes on a piano; there are only bad players. . . ."[3]

You might wreck your life by perverting the normal desires God gave you, but that doesn't change the fact that God created you. He expects you to satisfy your desires in the way He has designed. When you do, you are living life to the fullest.

God planted within us the desire to know Him. He created in us a hunger for the truth about Him. He gave us a godly discontent that will not be quieted until we find fellowship with Him.

After a surgeon repairs a defect in someone's heart valves, the patient suffers pain and gnawing discomfort through the weeks of recovery. But one day the patient is able to climb a flight of stairs once again, and he realizes that he can do it more easily than ever before. As the healing continues, he finds new strength to do simple activities that the heart defect had prevented him from doing. He is whole again, and he knows it is worth all the pain.

The same kind of thing happens to our spirits as we reach out for God. We feel pain and discomfort; but when we give our lives to Him, He makes us whole again. We become what He made us to be. And that brings ecstasy!

The God of Ecstasy
He Brings Order

Genesis 1:2 says: "The earth was without form, and void; and darkness was upon the face of the deep. And the Spirit of God moved upon the face of the waters." God brought order out of chaos. He put things in order. He preferred harmony and organization over discord and confusion.

He does the same today. He changes turbulence into peace and order. When He moves into your home, He quiets the confusion. When He enters your personal life, He straightens the troublesome wrinkles of your soul. He is doing the same kind of work today that He did on the first day of creation.

"Gipsy" Smith grew up in a band of gypsies that roamed the English countryside. He faced a number of temptations as he traveled from village to village, and he fell victim to many of them. He learned how to steal and lie to get his livelihood.

But he wanted to learn the English language, so he could leave gypsy life. When he was sixteen, his father gave him a Bible and a dictionary. The young man spent many nights reading by candlelight, trying to learn the subtle turns of English grammar.

The message of the Bible began speaking to the gypsy boy's mind. It laid conviction on his heart. One night he yielded his life to the Lord, praying, "Blessed Jesus, make my heart Thy home!"[4] And Christ did exactly that. He changed the boy's heart, so that he stopped lying and stealing and started preaching. In fact, "Gipsy" became one of England's best-known evangelists just after World War I. Christ rearranged his life.

If your life is mixed up and messed up, bring it to Jesus. He will create order out of disorder, peace out of turmoil, and contentment out of anxiety.

He Dispels the Darkness

As we read further in the Creation record, we find that God created the sun and moon "to divide the light from the darkness" (Gen. 1:18). This literally means that He separated day from night. He established the pattern of day and night to govern the earth's most basic activities.

But I believe this verse has a spiritual message, too. God still separates spiritual light from spiritual darkness. John says, "God is light and in Him is no darkness at all" (1 John 1:5). He cannot tolerate spiritual ignorance, moral indifference, or sin. Instead, He wants each heart to be filled with spiritual wisdom, purity, and power. If you are living in spiritual light, He wants you to avoid the darkness altogether; if you are living in darkness, He wants to drive it out with the light of His goodness.

Many years ago, a young Jewish man began attending worship services at the Olive Branch Mission in Chicago. He had heard about Jesus while attending a Jewish seminary in Cincinnati and, after reading a copy of the New Testament, he had accepted Jesus as the Messiah of his life. That decision cost him his place at the seminary, his friends, and even his family. For over two years he debated in his mind whether or not to forsake the Lord and return to his Jewish friends. He enjoyed the services at the mission, but he shied away from making a full commitment to Christ.

One night the preacher lady challenged him to kneel at the altar and pray for God's guidance. He made apologies and eased himself back toward the door. Others urged him to go forward, but he only made more excuses. Finally, a new convert took him by the hand and began pleading with him to get right with the Lord. Together they went to the altar and started to pray. Ralph Woodworth, a director of the mission, tells what happened:

> When he met God's terms, he jumped to his feet in an ecstasy of joy. He threw his arms around the fellow who had brought him to the altar. Then, rubbing his hands together, he exclaimed, "It is inexpressible!" He laid his hand over his heart and said, "There is some load gone!"[5]

That's the kind of feeling any person has when God penetrates his heart with the truth. Mr. Woodworth says in the title of his book that the gospel is like *Light in a Dark Place* and anyone God has brought out of a "dark place" will certainly testify to that.

He Forgives

Many people call John 3:16 the "golden text" of the New Testament. You probably can recite it from memory: "For God so loved the world that He gave His only begotten Son, that whoever believes in Him should not perish but have everlasting life." This is the bedrock of the gospel: God *loved* the world. He was not repaying a debt or setting up a shrewd business deal when He sent His Son into the world; He was expressing His love for mankind. Love is the essence of His nature. He loves us, no matter what happens.

I am glad God is not pure power, because power can destroy. The ancient Greeks and Romans believed some of their gods used brute force to exert their wishes. If an earthquake struck a city or a foreign nation invaded the frontier, the sages would say the gods must have ordered it. This is where we get the expression, "an act of God," which is how insurance companies explain natural disasters such as tornadoes or floods. But that is a pagan idea. The true God is not brutal, uncontrolled power. Aren't you glad?

I'm also happy to know that God is not *only* justice, because justice can do more harm than good. Read the Book of Leviticus and you will see what I mean. Strict justice demands an "eye for [an] eye, tooth for [a] tooth" (Lev. 24:20). But God sent His Son to earth to pay the penalty for our sin, in order that we may be justified before Him.

God is *love*. Isn't that thrilling? Love can look you straight in the eye and see all of your sins, and yet forgive you. Love can put aside all of your shortcomings and wrongdoings and make a fresh start. God can do this because of Jesus' sacrifice. Paul speaks of "God, who is rich in mercy, because of His great love with which He loved us, even when we were dead in trespasses" (Eph. 2:4,5). This loving, merciful God can look beyond our faults and love us in spite of ourselves. He can reach from the heights of heaven to give us eternal life, even though we deserve to die. He is a God of mercy and forgiveness.

We ought to be merciful as well. The Bible says, "Therefore be followers of God as dear children" (Eph. 5:1). Since God has made us His children, He expects us to follow His example in our daily lives. Mercy is one of His qualities that we should imitate most. With mercy in our hearts we can reach the heights of human fulfillment and ecstasy.

On the other hand, if we demand that everyone pay us their just dues, we will not be happy. An unmerciful person becomes hard and uncaring. Eventually, his soul dies within him. But when we follow God's example of mercy, we open our hearts to the needs of our neighbors. We become caring people. We find joy in helping others.

He Demands Obedience

After John baptized Jesus in the Jordan River and Jesus came up from the water, God said, "This is My beloved Son, in whom I am well-pleased" (Matt. 3:17). Why was He pleased? Because Jesus had obeyed Him and presented Himself to be baptized. God is always pleased with obedience.

Across the centuries, pagan religions have honored people who *disobeyed* their gods. The Greeks, the Romans, the Danes, the Saxons—these and many others told legends of people who were cunning enough to disobey their imaginary gods. They praised crafty, devious people. But this is not God's way. He expects us to follow Him wholeheartedly, without deceit.

An anonymous person penned these lines, which express so well the attitude a Christian should have toward his task:

> I am only one, but I am one.
> I cannot do everything, but
>   I can do something;
> And what I should do and can do,
>   by the grace of God
> I will do.[6]

God is pleased with this kind of attitude. Even if we don't accomplish all that we set out to do, our obedient attitudes will merit the Father's favor. He will smile on us and bless us.

By the way, another divine quality we ought to have is that of being well-pleased with other people. Disgruntled, complaining people can never have ecstasy. But people who appreciate and praise the good in others will find happiness bubbling up within themselves. Take time today to tell a neighbor, a co-worker, and your spouse how much you appreciate them. When you do, you will be expressing the sentiments of God's own Spirit.

He Is Worthy of Worship

The God we worship is a God of ecstasy. His very nature is full of happiness, and we become happier as we become more like Him. So our worship should have overtones of ecstasy. Notice how the Bible describes the worship of God's people:

> O clap your hands, all ye people; shout unto God with the voice of triumph (Ps. 47:1)

> Praise him upon the loud cymbals: praise him upon the high sounding cymbals (Ps. 150:5).

> Be filled with the Spirit, speaking to one another in psalms, hymns, and spiritual songs, singing and making melody in your heart to the Lord (Eph. 5:18,19).

We do not see much of this kind of worship today. God wants to give us ecstasy; and when He does, we will want lively, ecstatic worship instead of the dull, listless worship that has become so customary. Psalm 150:4 even says, "Praise him with the timbrel and dance." Dance unto the Lord! I know the devil has stolen dancing and perverted it, but it rightfully belongs to God. I dare say that we will dance in heaven; but there will be no dancing in hell, for there will be nothing to dance about!

One day the disciples of John asked Jesus, "Why don't your disciples fast?" Jesus said, "Can the friends of the bridegroom fast while the bridegroom is with them?" (Mark 2:19). This is beautiful. Jesus pictures Himself as the bridegroom who has come to woo His bride—the church. How can His disciples have sad, long faces at such a time as this? It's a time of rejoicing! It's a time to celebrate! We live in just such a time, and we should feel free to enter the happy spirit of the occasion whenever we worship the Lord!

The people of the Bible engaged in some of their most joyous worship during times of crisis. When God delivered the Israelites from bondage, they danced and played tambourines (Exod. 15:20). When Christ was born, the angels sang, "On earth peace, good will toward men"—even though the world certainly wasn't peaceful that night (Luke 2:14).

When the Holy Spirit established the church at Jerusalem, the disciples broke into rejoicing, even though they knew they would face persecution (cf. Acts 2:4). The Bible tells us that at the end of time, when all of God's people are invited to the marriage supper of the Lamb, there will be great rejoicing even though millions of souls are about to be thrown into the lake of fire (Rev. 19:9,17,18). All of this emphasizes that *worship is joyful because of the One who is being worshiped, not because of external circumstances*. When you surrender your life to the Lord, you should be happy to worship Him regardless of your circumstances. Joyful worship is the natural outpouring of a grateful heart.

Remember, God made joy before He placed the first man on the earth. God asked Job, "[Where wast thou] when the morning stars sang together, and all the sons of God shouted for joy?" (Job 38:7). Creation has always resounded with the joy of God's own Spirit. The stars made music and celebrated God's power long before man or woman composed the first hymn. The entire universe rejoices over the majesty of God.

Now God gives this ecstasy to human beings. His Spirit brought joy to Moses on Mount Sinai, to Ezekiel by the river of Babylon, and to David as he tended his sheep. God has ecstasy because of His marvelous creation, and He shares that ecstasy with everyone who has a receptive heart.

The Book of Revelation tells us that ecstasy will continue for ever and ever as God's saints worship Him in heaven:

> The throne of God and of the Lamb shall be in it, and His servants shall serve Him. And they shall see His face, and His name shall be on their foreheads. And there shall be no night there; they need no lamp nor light of the sun, for the Lord God gives them light. And they shall reign forever and ever (Rev. 22:3-5).

Can you imagine the singing and praising there will be in that New Jerusalem? What a glorious day that will be! What exultation and worship there will be! And we might as well begin it here and now, because the Savior has already entered our hearts. Let heaven come down into your prayer life; praise God with all your being. It's only natural for a Christian to praise Him.

The God of Ecstasy

There are too many sad people in the pews of our churches today. I have preached before dozens of congregations where a cloud of sadness and depression seemed to hang over the audience. God does not want that kind of worship. He sent His Son to bring joy to the world, and we ought to worship Him with uninhibited praise. "Let the redeemed of the Lord say so" (Ps. 107:2).

Chaplain Merlin R. Carouthers tells of attending a retreat with a friend from the Army. At first they felt intimidated by the worship services because people expressed their happiness so openly. Some worshipers clapped their hands; others shouted; others lifted their arms in joyful prayer. Chaplain Carouthers and his friend had never seen anything like this, but they decided to stay. They were curious.

As the hours passed, the two Army men reflected upon Christ's great love for them. They laid aside all thoughts of their personal problems and shortcomings, and the Lord's Holy Spirit came and filled them with ecstasy. "All my recent nagging doubts were swept away by a wave of joyous certainty," Col. Carouthers said later. "It was glorious! Never again could I doubt that Jesus Christ was who He said He was."[7]

You can have that "joyous certainty" about Christ. He is waiting to give you the peace and joy of His presence. It is the most thrilling experience you can ever know, and it will last as long as you leave your life in the hands of God, for He is the God of ecstasy.

Many people have a dull, monotonous worship life because they think worship is supposed to help them *receive* something from God. They drive home from a Sunday morning service and say, "I didn't get anything out of that!" Ministers add to the confusion when they say that the worship service is "a time to recharge your spiritual batteries." That's not entirely true. Maybe a person will get "recharged" by worshiping God, but that is not the *reason* for worshiping Him.

A Christian worships because he wants to *give* God everything that he is or hopes to be. Worship is a holy pouring-out of oneself. It's like shooting off fireworks; it consumes everything you have—but what a way to go! It's throwing yourself on the bonfire of His Spirit and letting the flames leap high. It's giving your entire being back to the Creator so He can use you however He wants. That's real worship!

God made us in such a way that we are happiest when we serve Him. We feel more vibrantly alive when we follow His will; we feel stronger, healthier, and more energetic when we let Him use our energies. That is our purpose. And when we fulfill our purpose, our hearts sing praises to Him.

Write down the happiest experience you had last week. Then your happiest experience of the past month. Then of the past three months. Study that list for a moment. Did those happy experiences come while you were obeying the Lord? Did they come *because* you were obeying Him? If they did, you were worshiping God, whether you realized it or not.

Even ironing clothes and tying shoelaces are worshipful things if you do them to serve the Lord. That's right! The most common chores can honor the Lord, if you do them with a Lord-loving attitude. Your sink can be your altar to Him and your desk can be your prayer rail, if you give yourself to Him there day by day.

Historians often say that the church grows stronger when it is persecuted. I believe that when Christians are free to go through the motions of worshiping God, they often take Him for granted. They are inclined to think they've done their duty by going to church twice on Sunday and dropping some money in the offering plate.

But when tyrants close the church doors, Christians realize how precious their relationship with God really is. They begin to savor every moment they spend with Him. They turn their thoughts to Him again and again and worship Him in the sanctuary of their hearts. Gradually they realize that worship is a round-the-clock experience. It's a matter of constant devotion to the Lord. When that truth begins to dawn upon them, they discover a joy they might never have found in their dull, indifferent worship services.

Thank God we are privileged to worship in a free country! I would never want to live in a land that bars the doors of its church buildings. But I think we should learn from Christians who do live in countries like that. We should realize that Jesus calls us to the most exciting, rewarding way of life we could ever have. He invites us to live in close communion with Him every minute of every day, and even while we sleep. He has come to bring us a rich, abundant life of serving Him. That's a precious experience we can have here and now, without waiting for hardship to force us into it.

Certain evangelists have told me that it's very difficult to lead a wealthy person to Christ because he has never had to depend on God for the basic needs of life. I think that's oversimplifying it, but there's some truth here—enough to make it sting! The world has millions of people who are wealthy but not rich, comfortable but not happy. They feel a void in their lives, but not enough to concern themselves about it. They may never search for God until tragedy strikes.

But think of the opportunity every one of us has right now, whether we're rich or poor, comfortable or not. The Lord wants us to join Him. He calls us to walk beside Him on the road of life. He invites us to find adventure, fulfillment, and peace. To put it simply, He invites us to find ecstasy as we follow the God of ecstasy. Will you accept His invitation?

IX

Men and Women Who Knew Ecstasy

Therefore, seeing we also are surrounded by so great a cloud of witnesses, let us lay aside every weight, and the sin which so easily ensnares us, and let us run with endurance the race that is set before us, looking to Jesus, the author and finisher of our faith, who for the joy that was set before Him endured the cross (Heb. 12:1,2).

It's easy to read about the saints of the Bible and say, "Well, they didn't have the kind of problems I have. If they did, they wouldn't have been so happy." Yet the people of Bible times had problems that were just as worrisome—if not more—as the ones we face today, and they knew victory. They were subject to death and taxes and obnoxious in-laws, just as we are. But they seemed happy—much happier than those around them.

In this chapter we will review the lives of some well-known people of the Bible to see why they were happy in the midst of their troubles. If these people had happiness, so can we.

Old Testament Ecstasy

Leaf through the pages of the Old Testament and you will find dozens of people who had ecstasy.

They seem to have had two basic kinds of joy, which we might call the *joy of worship* and the *joy of anticipation.*

I described the joy of worship in the previous chapter. It is a person's free, spontaneous praise of God. It might be expressed through a formal worship service, through an outburst of singing, or through any number of other ways. The joy of worship focuses on God the Creator, offering Him the overflow of a grateful heart. It is the most common form of ecstasy, and we see it emerge in every Book of the Old Testament.

Miriam

For example, look at the ecstatic worship Miriam expressed when God delivered her people from the Egyptians (Exod. 15:20). Miriam was Moses' older sister, the one who had watched him floating on the Nile in a reed basket when he was a baby (Exod. 2:4). She knew firsthand how God had led Moses to become the deliverer of the Hebrews, and I'm sure that all those memories came flooding into her mind as she watched the Egyptian army drowning in the Red Sea. She felt a wave of joy surging through her entire being. God had performed miracle after miracle to save her people—to save *her*— and she just couldn't keep quiet about it. So Miriam picked up a tambourine and danced around the camp, singing praises to God.

Miriam's song is the first hymn recorded in the Bible. Notice how the words express her delight in the Lord:

> Sing ye to the Lord, for he hath triumphed gloriously; the horse and his rider hath he thrown into the sea (Exod. 15:21).

Men and Women Who Knew Ecstasy

David

Another good example of the joy of worship is found in David's life. If we look at his life from a cynical standpoint, we can find many reasons for him to be bitter toward God. He was the "baby" of the family, so he had to stay home when his brothers went off to war. He was anointed to be king, but he had to keep it a secret. King Saul was jealous of David and tried to kill him on several occasions, but the Lord would not let David run away.

If you or I were in David's sandals, we could find plenty of reasons to complain. But David didn't dwell on that; he thought instead about how good God was to him. Many times his gratitude erupted into singing and dancing. Even when he was king, David was not ashamed to take his lyre and strum a chorus of praise to the Lord.

The Book of Psalms gives us dozens of songs he composed to worship his Lord. Sometimes the lyrics dip into moods of sorrow or discouragement, but they always come back to a theme of triumph and joy. I think it's interesting that the king of Israel, who probably experienced more pressure and anxiety than anyone else in the realm, still had the ecstasy of worship. In this respect, David is a good example for all of us.

In one of his Psalms, David said, "They that sow in tears shall reap in joy" (Ps. 126:5). He certainly had plenty of tears in his lifetime, because of all his disappointments and failures. But in spite of all that, he knew life had a harvest of joy.

David said that the Lord was his Shepherd (Ps. 23:1). In other words, he knew the Lord cared for him and protected him, like a shepherd guards his sheep. This is one of the most beautiful statements in the entire Bible. Matters of state, matters of war, and matters of personal conflict troubled David, but he could still say that God "restoreth my soul" (Ps. 23:3). When problems or sorrows came, God restored David's will to live. No matter what threatened to tear down David's faith, God was ready to build it up again.

And here's another interesting comment from David: "Thou preparest a table before me in the presence of mine enemies" (Ps. 23:5). David would not let even his enemies draw his attention away from God; he would not allow conflict to sap his joy; he would not let his tormentors get the best of him.

Everybody has enemies. Even ministers do. Once I was flying along in an airliner, making notes for a sermon, and when I looked up for a moment the woman across the aisle stuck out her tongue at me! She did not know who I was or anything about me, but she was hostile to me. You do not have to hurt anyone to make enemies; just begin following Jesus, and Satan will throw enemies across your path. But you do not need to let enemies steal your joy. David didn't.

Hezekiah

King Hezekiah of Judah was another Old Testament person who knew the joy of worship. Second Chronicles 29 paints a colorful picture of a worship service in Hezekiah's time. The kingdom of Israel had just fallen to the Assyrians, and Hezekiah invited the refugees to an extended Passover celebration. Can you imagine that? His most important ally was defeated, the enemy armies were just a few miles away, and Hezekiah wanted to have a worship service! The Bible says, "The song of the Lord began . . . and all the congregation worshiped, and the singers sang, and the trumpeters sounded: . . . and they bowed their heads and worshipped" (2 Chron. 29:27–30).

Hezekiah was not going to let a war spoil his worship. He was not about to put on sackcloth and start wailing about how terrible conditions were. God was still in control of the world, so Hezekiah was happy. It was natural to celebrate.

Ezra and Nehemiah

Ezra and Nehemiah faced similar hardships after the Babylonian Exile. With Persia's permission. they led the Jewish people back to the Promised Land to reestablish the nation of Israel. The city of Jerusalem lay in ruins. The temple was a heap of rubble.

The Jews' first task was to build a new wall around the city, to keep them safe from intruders. The work was hard and slow, and people who had settled near Jerusalem during the Exile tried to hinder the project. But Ezra and Nehemiah urged their people to continue.

Finally, the day came when the Jews were ready to dedicate the new walls. They brought out their cymbals and trumpets for a festival of praise to God. Scripture says that "[they] wept with a loud voice; and many shouted aloud for joy: So that the people could not discern the noise of the shout of joy from the noise of the weeping of the people . . . and the noise was heard afar off" (Ezra 3:12,13).

I would say those people had ecstasy, wouldn't

you? I can just imagine Nehemiah, a court servant of the king of Persia, placing the stones in the wall of Jerusalem. Sweat ran down his face; his hands were sore and calloused; he carried a sword for protection, often carrying a stone in one hand and his sword in the other. Yet Nehemiah was happy. Remember that he told his friends, "The joy of the Lord is your strength" (Neh. 8:10). He glorified God as he worked, and the joy of worship made him strong to do the task.

So this was one kind of ecstasy we find among Old Testament people: the ecstasy of worshiping God. But if we look closely, we will see another kind of joy: the joy of anticipating the future.

Israel passed through some deep, troublesome waters in her history. Again and again, the people turned away from God to worship the pagan idols of the Canaanites, and God punished them. Great empires were rising in the east, threatening to seize the narrow strip of land where the Israelites lived. Their army was weak; their politicians were foolish; and they were at the mercy of forces they could not control.

Yet they had hope. Even in their gloomiest hours, they looked for deliverance in the future. God had promised to send a messiah who would break their shackles and make them a powerful nation; they could not doubt that promise. So beneath Israel's heartbreaking story of apostasy and failure, we see a thread of happy anticipation.

Isaiah

Isaiah condemned his people for their idolatrous and immoral living; he predicted that Judah would collapse before the armies of King Nebuchadnezzar. And yet he saw a brighter day on the horizon. "The ransomed of the Lord shall return," he said, "and come to Zion with songs and everlasting joy upon their heads: they shall obtain joy and gladness, and sorrow and sighing shall flee away" (Isa. 35:10).

Isaiah knew that God had chosen His people to bring redemption into the world. Despite all their sin, they would pass through the fire of testing and emerge stronger for it. Isaiah was like a master chess player who sees more than his next move; he looked beyond Judah's punishment and pain to the victory that waited on the other side. And what he saw made him happy.

Jeremiah

Jeremiah did the same. His sermons were full of impending doom and destruction. He warned that the people of Judah should accept Nebuchadnezzar as their friend instead of trying to get the Egyptians to help fight him. But the prophet's words went unheeded until Nebuchadnezzar's army stormed the city of Jerusalem. Even then, the Jewish leaders took Jeremiah's advice with a large dose of skepticism. Zedekiah, the governor whom Nebuchadnezzar appointed, tried again to curry favor with the Egyptians. Jeremiah saw trouble coming, and he said so. That earned him a prison cell.

But like Isaiah, Jeremiah could see beyond the agony that was about to come. He was excited about the future, and he shared his excitement with anyone who cared to listen. In the shadow of prison, he cried:

> Thus saith the Lord; Refrain thy voice from weeping, and thine eyes from tears: for thy work shall be rewarded, saith the Lord; and they shall come again from the land of the enemy" (Jer. 31:16).

God is speaking through Jeremiah here, saying, "It is not time for weeping. See My deliverance, My power, My anointing, My blessing, and walk in ecstasy." What a tremendous message!

I have often heard Bible commentators call Jeremiah the "prophet of doom." Certainly, there is a strong mood of foreboding in his prophecy. But there is also hope. There is joyful anticipation. There is the ecstasy of knowing that God will triumph and His people will triumph with Him. In the midst of devastating change, Isaiah and Jeremiah pointed their people toward the future, because they knew the future belonged to God.

New Testament Ecstasy

Now let us turn our attention to the New Testament, where we also find many people expressing ecstasy. We notice that several of these people have the joy of worship or the joy of anticipation, just as their ancestors did. But another kind of joy comes on the scene here: the *joy of fulfillment*. Men and women rejoiced to see God fulfilling the promises of His covenant; this is one of the most inspiring aspects of the New Testament.

Zacharias

In Luke 1 we read that an angel appeared to a priest named Zacharias and promised that he would have a son. "And you will have joy and gladness," the angel said, "and many will rejoice at his birth" (Luke 1:14). The angel was announcing the birth of John the Baptist, the forerunner who Isaiah said would prepare the way for the Messiah (Isa. 40:3).

This took Zacharias by surprise. He was an elderly man, and his wife was well past the age of childbearing. He questioned the angel how this could happen. Since Zacharias had not believed the angel's words, the angel took away Zacharias's voice, saying he would speak again when the baby was born. It all happened as the angel had said it would. So what did Zacharias do? The Bible says, "Immediately his mouth was opened and his tongue loosed, and he spoke and praised God" (Luke 1:64). He knew the joy of fulfillment.

Shepherds

Read on in the Gospel of Luke and you will find the account of the shepherds who were tending their sheep in the hills near Bethlehem the night Jesus was born. An angel suddenly appeared and said, "Do not be afraid, for behold, I bring you good tidings of great joy which will be to all people" (Luke 2:10).

As the angel described the baby who had just been born in Bethlehem, the shepherds realized He was the Messiah. So they hurried into town, and found the baby Jesus lying in a manger of hay, as the angel had predicted. "And the shepherds returned, glorifying and praising God for all the things that they had heard and seen" (Luke 2:20). They knew the joy of fulfillment.

Notice that the news of Jesus' birth would bring "great joy which will be to all people." This is a marvelous statement. It reemphasizes that every human being is entitled to ecstasy. God has given us His Son, who entitles us to walk with a sprightly gait and hold our heads high in confidence.

The news of Jesus Christ is the best news this world has ever heard. It means God has kept His word of promise. It means happiness for today and hope for tomorrow. It means that ecstasy is now the natural condition of humanity. Jesus Christ came "to seek and to save that which was lost" (Luke 19:10), so you have no reason to be lost, and no reason to lose the joy that is rightfully yours. You should have ecstasy. If you don't, someone must have stolen it from you. Get it back!

Palm Sunday Crowds

This is the joy of fulfillment—the joy of realizing that God keeps His Word. We see it again on Palm Sunday, when Jesus rode triumphantly into Jerusalem. Crowds lined the street and shouted, "Blessed is the King who comes in the name of the Lord!" (Luke 19:38). They knew that Jesus fit the prophets' description of their long-awaited Messiah, so they gave free rein to their ecstatic feelings.

The embittered Pharisees asked Jesus to quiet the noisy throng, but He said, "I tell you that if these should keep silent, the stones would immediately cry out" (Luke 19:40). There is no way to restrain the joy of people who see God at work in their lives—what's inside must come out somehow.

We see dozens of Christian books about self-confidence, self-understanding, and self-therapy; but how many books are there about contemplating God and His deeds? Seldom do pastors or evangelists talk about *adoration*—marvelling at

God's majesty. Yet that is how the shepherds, the wise men, and the Palm Sunday crowds responded to Jesus.

In our modern world, we have forgotten how to adore Him; we seldom know the joy of fulfillment. We should learn how to enjoy God again. We should pause in front of the everyday miracles He places along our path. When we watch Him fulfilling His promises, our lives begin to blossom in a bouquet of joy. It's a glorious experience.

Many men and women of the New Testament knew the joy of worship, which is closely related to the joy of fulfillment. The latter is our response to what God *does,* while the former is our response to who God *is.* A Christian should have both.

Christians at Pentecost

All kinds of people gathered in an upper room on the day of Pentecost; only their love of Christ brought them together. Eleven were Jesus' select group of followers. One was Jesus' mother, Mary. Another was Jesus' close friend, Mary Magdalene. They came from different family backgrounds, different social strata, and different occupations. Yet the Holy Spirit moved them in a mighty way, uniting them and filling them with an intense desire to spread the gospel. These 120 people had such ecstasy that strangers who passed by exclaimed, "My! These people must be drunk with wine!"

Peter rose to defend them. "Wait a minute!" I can imagine him saying, "It's only nine in the morning. And this Jerusalem wine wouldn't make anybody drunk, unless they drank it all day. No, these people are *happy.* They have received what the prophet Joel predicted when he said, 'I will pour out my spirit upon all flesh; and your sons and daughters shall prophesy . . .' " (cf. Acts 2:1–17; Joel 2:28–32). In other words, they were worshiping in the joy of the Holy Spirit.

If only every Christian had this ecstasy! Our lives would be so full of it that even our neighbors would notice the change. Remember Peter's words: "Though now you do not see Him, yet believing, you rejoice with joy unspeakable and full of glory" (1 Pet. 1:8). I cannot explain this joy; I cannot define it. I can only tell you that it flows out of a Christian's innermost being as he savors the personality of God.

In true worship, a person completely abandons himself to the person and presence of God, like a swimmer abandons himself to the ocean. It is an experience that totally absorbs the worshiper and changes his life. Dr. James F. White has said:

> The love of God exists independently of our worship. But in worship we rediscover and respond to this love in such a way that it can change the rest of our lives.[1]

At Pentecost, the people learned this. One glorious moment of worship sent them out to serve the Lord. It filled them with an ecstatic zeal to preach the gospel. You see, the joy of worship is not a static, self-centered thing; it inspires a person to give himself more completely to the Lord. Otherwise it would not be worship but a kind of spiritual thrill-seeking.

Peter praised his Christian friends for their worshipful attitude toward Christ, "whom having not seen you love. Though now you do not see Him," Peter said, "yet believing, you rejoice with joy unspeakable and full of glory" (1 Pet. 1:8). Only in the Spirit can we come to know Christ. None of us has seen Him personally. *But we know Him,* and our spirits testify to that fact by pouring out "joy unspeakable," as Peter said. And it is thrilling to meet other Christians who have this worshipful joy.

The Apostles

Paul met with the elders of the Ephesian church, encouraging them to be faithful to the Lord and continue their work, despite the trouble that had overtaken him. "None of these things move me," he said, "nor do I count my life dear to myself, so that I may finish my race with joy . . ." (Acts 20:24). Paul had the joy of knowing he was in God's presence— the joy of worship.

Acts 8 tells us that an evangelist named Philip went to Samaria, the capital city of the old kingdom of Judah, and preached the gospel of Jesus Christ. Imagine how strange this message sounded to people who lived in this stronghold of Jewish tradition. Philip said this man Jesus was the Son of God, and He had ascended to heaven. The very idea! It's a wonder the city elders didn't throw the preacher man into jail.

But the Bible says, "There was great joy in that city" (Acts 8:8). *Great joy!* Why? Because the Holy Spirit convicted their hearts with Philip's message, and they realized it was true. Wouldn't you like to have lived in that city, where so many people were praising God and responding eagerly to the gospel? What a grand place to live!

The New Testament tells us that early Christians also knew the joy of anticipation. Like the patriarchs and prophets who anticipated the Messiah's coming, the Christians anticipated His return. They knew Christ would come back to judge and rule the world, and that very thought filled them with happiness.

Today it is very common to hear people speak about Jesus' return with fear and anxiety in their voices. Even Christians talk about it with a tremor of doom. We are so preoccupied with the tribulation and suffering that will fall upon the world that we forget about the victory Christ will bring. He is coming to claim His own people—that's us! He is coming to save sinners who have repented from their sin. *That's us!* He is coming to take the "redeemed of the Lord" away from all suffering and sorrow. THAT'S US! We ought to be excited about His coming; we ought to be eager to see Him come; we ought to be happy to know He's coming soon.

Jesus said the world will suffer great tribulations just before He returns. "Nation will rise against nation," He said. "There will be great earthquakes in various places, and famines and pestilences; and there will be fearful sights and great signs from heaven" (Luke 21:10,11).

That's an awesome forecast, isn't it? But notice what Jesus told us to do when these things happen. He did not tell us to huddle in some sort of Doomsday fallout shelter. Nor did He tell us to put on mourning clothes and start wailing about our pitiful situation. No! He said, "Now when these things begin to happen, look up and lift up your heads, because your redemption draws near" (Luke 21:28). Hallelujah! What a breathtaking sight that will be!

In John's vision of the last days, he saw tribulations plaguing the people of earth. He saw the world powers collapse. He saw economic chaos and financial ruin. He saw people throwing dust on their heads and wailing in agony because their world was falling apart. But he also saw a great multitude of God's people in heaven, and here's what he heard them say:

> Alleluia! For the Lord God Omnipotent reigns! Let us be glad and rejoice and give Him glory, for the marriage of the Lamb has come, and His wife has made herself ready (Rev. 19:6,7).

"His wife" refers to the church, the bride of Christ (cf. Eph. 5:25–27; Rev. 21:2). This multitude in heaven is talking about the "household of God" (Eph. 2:19). In other words, *they are talking about us*. The day Christ returns will be our great wedding day—the day the church goes home to be with Him. It's a day I am looking forward to, and I hope you are, too.

This is the joy of anticipation. The New Testament sings with it. The anticipation of Christ's return is enough to make even the most dour Christian leap for joy. It's an event that will hold more for the Christian than any experience he has ever known. Why shouldn't he long for it? In heaven there will be no tears, no death, no sickness, no despair. There will be only endless anthems of praise, magnifying God.

Our Privilege

At the beginning of this chapter I quoted a familiar passage from the Letter to the Hebrews. Take a moment to read it again.

I want to draw your attention to the phrase that

says "so great a cloud of witnesses" (Heb. 12:1). That's what we've been talking about in this chapter—the cloud of witnesses from all the ages past who testify that there is joy in the Lord. Their testimony is very precious to us, because it reminds us of our great privilege in the Lord—the privilege of joy.

God has given us ecstasy, just as He gave it to the people of Bible times. Let's keep it alive. Let's share it with the people around us. As every day brings us closer to heaven, let's shout the praises of God in our hearts.

X

The Enemies of Ecstasy

Fight the good fight with all thy might!
  Christ is thy strength and Christ thy right;
Lay hold on life and it shall be
  Thy joy and crown eternally.

—John S. B. Monsell[1]

How nice it would be to live in a world where nothing distracted us from God; where we could chart our course to heaven without any detours; where living in fellowship with God was the normal, accepted way of life. How nice it would be!

But we don't live in that kind of world. Many things threaten to draw us away from God and squelch the ecstasy of our fellowship with Him. We face many enemies of ecstasy—most of them subtle and hidden. But they are potent enemies nevertheless. We need to identify them as enemies and understand them as such, so that we can resist them when they try to disrupt our lives. The apostle John said:

Do not love the world or the things in the world. If anyone loves the world, the love of the Father is not in him. For all that is in the world—the lust of the flesh,

> the lust of the eyes, and the pride of life—is not of the
> Father but is of the world. And the world is passing
> away, and the lust of it; but he who does the will of God
> abides forever (1 John 2:15–17).

In this passage, John puts his finger on the three
basic forms that the enemies of ecstasy may take.
He calls them "the lust of the flesh," "the lust of the
eyes," and "the pride of life." Just what does he
mean by these phrases?

• *The lust of the flesh*. This term encompasses all
the sensuous desires known to man, whether they
be illicit sexual desires, unbridled appetites for
food or drink, or any other kind of self-serving desires. "The lust of the flesh" is an unrestrained drive
for self-satisfaction. It may express itself in a
greedy struggle to get the "creature comforts" for
oneself, disregarding the needs of everyone else. It
may also express itself in some unnatural in-
dulgence of the physical appetites—gluttony,
promiscuity, and so on. This is "the lust of the
flesh" in its most repulsive form. Yet this kind of
lust affects other people in less obvious ways.

For example, some people are tempted to drive
big, luxurious cars, even though they have no large
family. Others are tempted to spend "windfall"
money on an exotic vacation or a chic new ward-
robe. Still others are tempted to take some "sick
days" from work to do a little fishing or stretch out
in the hammock. We should not laugh at these
things, because they are not trivial. They are common examples of "the lust of the flesh."

• *The lust of the eyes*. It may seem difficult to
separate this from "the lust of the flesh," but there

is an important difference here. The commentator Harvey J.S. Blaney explains:

> *The lust of the eyes* is unlawful, "prurient curiosity." This lust involves what one does not have. *The lust of the flesh* involves what one has and uses to evil ends.[2]

So "the lust of the eyes" may not be outwardly expressed; it is a greedy longing that a person may entertain within his mind, yet never act upon.

At other times, a person may plot to get the object of his desire. If he has entertained this lust long enough, he may put aside all moral scruples to get what he wants. He may lie, steal, even kill to get it. So "the lust of the eyes" is not an innocent pastime.

Jesus said, "Whoever looks at a woman to lust for her has already committed adultery with her in his heart" (Matt. 5:28). That's what "the lust of the eyes" will do; it will make your heart a laboratory for sin experiments that you might never try in real life. But Christ considers experiments that you carry out in your mind to be sinful, too.

● *The pride of life.* One commentator defines this as "empty trust in possessions."[3] That certainly is a part of it—a person's boasting about what he has acquired and what he has achieved in life. But it is more than that. "The pride of life" includes every effort to trust in human ability and ingenuity, rather than trusting in God.

Have you heard the fairy tale about the cobbler who killed seven houseflies with one swat? The man was so pleased that he made himself a special belt that said, *"Seven with one blow,"* and he wore it wherever he went. People were impressed, because they thought he'd killed seven men with one blow. So they were extra careful not to offend the proud little man.

We chuckle over the story, but it reveals a serious truth about human nature. We are tempted to trust ourselves rather than God. We tend to give ourselves the credit for success, rather than give it to God. This is "the pride of life," pure and simple. John says we should avoid it at all costs.

All these things can cripple our spiritual lives. They can build a wall between us and God. They can cut off the flow of ecstasy that God wants to pour out upon us. So they are enemies of ecstasy.

Some Enemies Identified

Now that we've seen how the enemies operate, let's see how some of the enemies appear. We can't expect every temptation to be labeled like a bottle of poison; the enemies of ecstasy don't just walk up to us on the street, wearing bright red shirts that say The Lust of the Flesh or The Pride of Life. No, they come wrapped more attractively than that, and we must be careful to identify them for what they really are.

Transgression

Transgression is a violation of the law of God. It means that a person wants to do something besides what God has told him to do, so he follows his own priorities. Guilt is the inevitable result. Scripture says, "The wicked flee when no man pursueth: but the righteous are bold as a lion" (Prov. 28:1). This nervous guilt will rob you of ecstasy.

Some people rarely sleep because they have such a keen sense of guilt. They know that if the police catch them, they are sunk! So they are wary about life. They are afraid to let down their guard. They think they are being watched every minute. What kind of a life is that?

The only solution to this predicament is to come back to obeying God and the laws He has ordained. A person must stop breaking God's law—and man's law that is based on God's law—in order to find contentment and peace.

Isaiah said, "The wicked are like the troubled sea, when it cannot rest, whose waters cast up mire and dirt. There is no peace, saith my God, to the wicked" (Isa. 57:20,21). What a stunning picture of the guilt-ridden life! It is like the churning waters of an ocean in a storm, which toss seaweed and debris upon the beaches. The turmoil of a guilty person's heart brings up all the filthy thoughts and desires that lie deep within. The greater the anxiety and turmoil, the more filthiness comes out. It is a vicious cycle that can destroy a person who refuses to follow God.

Selfishness

A selfish person cannot be happy, because he can never be satisfied. The Bible tells us, "He that is greedy of gain troubleth his own house" (Prov. 15:27). Everyday experience shows this is true: Some people are so greedy that they do not give their own family proper food, clothing, and shelter. While trying to make life more secure, they consume life itself.

The gospel songwriter Gloria Gaither comments

that our society seems obsessed with greed and acquisitiveness. She writes:

> "Freedom" has undergone reverse evolution back to the barbaric struggle to preserve oneself with no regard for the needs of others.
> Freedom has become distorted to mean the right of a man to thrust a greedy fist into the grabbag of our culture and take whatever and as much as he can make off with. Now, nearly too late, a few are beginning to awaken to the tragedy of our loss. . . .[4]

We see evidence of this nearly everywhere we turn. Fraud in government, "get-rich-quick" deals, stinginess in giving to the church—these and many more signs point to a strong undercurrent of greed that is pulling us away from God. It is the cause of much unhappiness and discontent in our land. Economists try all sorts of formulas to combat inflation, but its number one cause is *greed*. Government has not been able to curb greed, and as long as it runs unchecked, it will bring misery.

A person lives on this earth for sixty or seventy years, and then he dies and someone else gets what he had. Study the tombstones in a cemetery, and you will see that many people don't have their possessions very long. Life goes so quickly! No sooner was Picasso buried than his family started fighting over his estate; the French government claimed most of it for taxes. That's life! But so often people ignore the realities of life, and they spend all their years trying to hoard up something for themselves. And in the process, they lose their joy.

Once I was dining at the home of a millionaire. After dinner, the millionaire's wife took me aside to the music room and said, "There is a gun in my handbag. I intended after dinner tonight to blow my brains out." I talked and prayed with her for an hour and a half, trying to divert her plans. It was a very sad experience.

I have known dozens of other people who feel the same way. They have spent their lives heaping up money and other material gain, but they are still not satisfied. They have not found happiness. They are beginning to realize that "looking out for number one" destroyed their happiness.

Pride

A proud person is never happy, even though he may claim to be. He tries to display his abilities in every situation, because inwardly he feels clumsy and insecure. Even when he succeeds, he feels like a failure, and he tries to cover his feelings with boisterous, arrogant behavior. The Book of Proverbs speaks to this person's situation, too; it says, "A man's pride shall bring him low: but honor shall uphold the humble in spirit" (Prov. 29:23). This Scripture verse vividly spells out the contrast between a proud person, who has false prestige, and a humble person, who has honor.

Pride caused Satan to lose his place in heaven. Once he was one of God's trusted lieutenants, an angel who served the Most High. But he said to himself, "I will ascend into heaven, I will exalt my throne above the stars of God" (Isa. 14:13). He wanted to be equal with God! And through his pride, he lost everything.

Joyce Landorf, an author and popular speaker, tells of a harrowing experience she had in a private plane. She had just spoken at a remote military base in California and was having a hard time making connections on a commercial flight home. A young Christian pilot offered to charter a small, single-engine plane and take her there. Joyce agreed. But from the moment they climbed into the cockpit, she saw that she'd made a mistake.

The young man ignored the normal safety procedures, neglected to file a flight plan, and flew low across the hills at breakneck speed. All the while, he gave her a running commentary of his "near-miss" experiences and landing mishaps. They encountered some rain and fog, but the pilot made no radio contact until Joyce insisted on it. His cocksure attitude dismissed any notion of danger. Joyce vowed never to fly with him again. She wrote later:

> I want a pilot who is not too big, too important, too experienced, or too seasoned to be obedient. I have learned that when a plane has crashed and the investigators lay the blame on "pilot error," it almost always means a pilot has disobeyed or failed to regard some long-standing, often simple rule.[5]

All of us have known people who wreck their lives in the same way. They are so blinded by their own pride that they cannot accept guidance or advice from anyone else—not even from God. So they stumble along on their own power and never know the ecstasy of being guided and empowered by God.

Hatred

It is impossible to have hate and ecstasy in the same person at the same time, but many people live as though it is. As I travel across the United States and speak in evangelistic meetings, I find that nearly everyone dislikes someone else. People make snide remarks about their in-laws, their children, or their work supervisors. Everyone has been hurt at one time or another, and often a person pushes the hurt deep within himself, where it grinds and growls all the time. It's just waiting to get revenge on someone else.

Until you get rid of the hate in your heart, you cannot know the ecstasy I've been talking about. God in all of His holiness is able to forgive someone who wrongs Him; so when you refuse to forgive, you are trying to imply that you are holier than God. Don't be ridiculous! You do no one a favor by nursing a grudge. It is better to love people and risk being taken advantage of, than to hate them and let the hatred gnaw at your heart.

Of course, many *things* deserve to be hated. I hate sin and evil of every kind. I hate alcoholism. I hate divorce. I hate witchcraft and mysticism. But I love the people who have fallen victim to all these things. If my dearest friend were dying of cancer I would keep on loving him, even though I hated the cancer that was claiming his life. That's the same attitude I have toward sin.

But even here, I know that the struggle is God's and not my own. I don't let the victories of sin discourage me, because I know that God will overcome sin in the end. I am one of His instruments in the battle, so I am utterly opposed to the enemy. But I don't allow my hatred of sin to make me a bitter, vindictive preacher. Sin is going to be defeated, regardless of any temporary gains it makes today. I'm not going to fume and fret about the progress of the battles, because I know God will win the war.

Irritability

If you are constantly irritable, you certainly are not happy. Do all sorts of things bother you— financial problems, family obligations, politics? Do even trivial things get your dander up? Do you complain about the weather or the amount of time you had to wait for a signal light? A church bulletin board I noticed recently displayed this message: *Ulcers come from mountain-climbing over mole hills.*

That pretty well describes the life of an irritable person; he is always making much ado about nothing. Eventually, it affects his health—physically, mentally, and spiritually.

An irritable disposition points to hidden problems in a person's life. Perhaps he doesn't feel satisfied with his job, his home, or some other facet of his life that he does not feel free to criticize, so he "takes it out" on everything and everyone else. Perhaps he feels like a failure in some vital area of his life, so he snaps at other people. Or perhaps he simply is not at peace with God, and he is lashing out in frustration. Whatever the reason, an irritable person makes life miserable for himself and for the people around him.

Fear

All of us experience pangs of fear from time to time. Fear can be a healthy impulse. It keeps children from crossing a busy street. It makes us careful about walking along steep cliffs or other places of physical danger. Fear is a God-given emotion.

But some people's fears are abnormally intense or prolonged, and others have groundless fears that make them unusually timid. These kinds of fear will thwart the ecstasy of living. A person trembling with fear is not happy, and God certainly does not expect us to live in constant fear.

The psalmist said, "The Lord is my light and my salvation; whom shall I fear? the Lord is the strength of my life; of whom shall I be afraid?" (Ps. 27:1). Isn't that a great affirmation? Every one of us can say that when we walk with God. When fear begins creeping into our lives, we can say, "I reject you! I will not be afraid! I will trust the Lord!" Then peace will come into our lives once again, and joy will begin to flow.

B. J. Cauthren was a missionary to China until the Communists seized control in 1945. Since then, he has served as an executive with several Baptist missionary agencies, and finally as executive secretary of the Foreign Missions Board. Recently he gave these words of advice to young missionaries about to leave for the foreign field:

> As you go, do not look at the swelling rivers, at the clouds that gather on the horizon, at real or imagined dangers, but turn your eyes upon Jesus. You will find that he has a way of turning every situation into an opportunity. You can stand in the midst of it and say in your soul: "This is what my Lord foresaw when he called me to follow him."[6]

An old hymn says, "He's the Christ of every crisis," and my years of experience have certainly proved it to be true. No matter what problems we face—or imagine we face—Christ can help us meet the challenge. If we are His, we have no need to be afraid. We can defeat the enemy of fear by placing our trust in Him.

Novelist H. G. Wells said, "I am alone and I have never been happy!" His despair colored everything he wrote. But thousands of people would add their "amen" to what Wells said. They feel lonely, uncared for, and neglected. Loneliness is one of the greatest heartaches of our time.

I can honestly say that I never feel lonely. I have visited the mountains of Tibet by myself; I have lived among Indian tribes in the jungles of Brazil for five months at a time; I have drifted down a tropical river for days and days on a decrepit river boat. But through all of those experiences I did not feel lonely.

Loneliness is a disease of the spirit. Self-pity causes loneliness, and self-pity comes from self-interest. So to get rid of loneliness, you need to get rid of the selfish, ego-centered spirit within you. God can help you do that.

Many people find all the fellowship they want through prayer. They communicate with God and are happy, even though they have few other friends. Others are so full of the friendship of God that they begin their day by walking up to a total stranger, giving him a gospel tract, and saying, "Good morning!" They are eager to share the spirit they have, because God has blessed them with an abundance of joy.

Larry Poland is an executive with Campus Crusade for Christ. He tells of starting to attend a certain church and encountering a very gruff, hostile man. Larry was determined to express his love to the man, so he invited him out to lunch. At first, the lunch conversation was tense. But gradually the other man relaxed and talked in friendly terms. As they left the restaurant, he took Larry aside and said: "You know, people think I'm a grouchy old guy. But I don't mean to be. I really thank you for this lunch today, and it's been wonderful getting to know you—to know you as a brother in Christ."[7]

This situation illustrated an old proverb that says, "If you want a friend—be one!" People often feel lonely and neglected because they have withdrawn to themselves, leaving no room for anyone else to share their lives. This raises a barrier to God's ecstasy, because it cuts off their relationships with the rest of God's children. Don't let it happen to you.

Kill the Giants

We have identified seven enemies of ecstasy. There are many more, of course. If you choose to indulge in illicit sex, lying, stealing, or any number of things that are ungodly and unlawful, you will lose all the joy God wants you to have. It's as simple as that. Your life will be filled with remorse and condemnation, and you will find the so-called pleasures of these things empty and meaningless.

God does not want you to have a life of failure! He does not want you to wallow in frustration and guilt! He is the God of ecstasy, the God of joy, and He wants you to have the joy He intended for man from the beginning of time.

I am fascinated by the story of David and Goliath. Every time I read it, I find more principles that can be applied to the Christian life. For one thing, think about the threat Goliath posed to the army of Israel. He was a giant. He was a strong, ferocious fighter.

No one in the Israelite camp could match his size and strength, and so he challenged them to send out someone to fight him.

Now Goliath could not have fought against all the Israelites single-handedly; even he knew that. But if one man dared to come out against him, Goliath would have the advantage. The enemies of ecstasy are the same way. They challenge you to go out and "take them on," to test your strength against them. Only a fool would try it alone.

But David went out with the Lord, and he won the contest. He certainly was no match for Goliath's size and power, but he let God use what he had. That was enough. You cannot kill your spiritual enemies on your own; but if you trust God to guide your battle against them, you will win the contest.

With His help, you can kill the giants that threaten to take away your ecstasy. Then you will walk in great joy before the Lord.

XI
Ecstasy Is Yours Forever

When the sun of bliss is beaming
Light and love upon my way,
From the cross the radiance streaming
Adds more luster to the day.

Bane and blessing, pain and pleasure,
By the cross are sanctified;
Peace is there that knows no measure,
Joys that thru all time abide.

—John Bowring[1]

When you give a boy his first pocket knife, there is just one thing he wants to ask: "Is it mine for good?" He does not want to enjoy the gift, grow fond of it, and then have to give it back. He wants to know that it's his to keep.

We ask the same question about ecstasy, the God-given joy that we find through Jesus Christ. Is it ours forever? Or is it only an occasional experience that comes and goes, no matter what we do?

Throughout this book, I have said that God created us to have ecstasy. We have examined several Scripture passages that say so, and we have looked at the lives of Christians who know it is so. I believe God made all living things to have ecstasy. I believe that a bird finds ecstasy in its freedom to fly. I believe a fish finds ecstasy in its ability to swim. And I believe that God wants human beings to know ecstasy as they enter into full communion with Jesus Christ, their Savior and Lord.

Our mouths were made to smile. Our eyes were made to sparkle and shine. Our feet were made to carry us along with a lively bounce. Everything about our bodies testifies that we were made to look and feel and *be* happy.

Many of us spend our lives searching for ecstasy, only to find a little glimpse of happiness now and then. When we have these experiences we are glad. But straightaway something interferes with our lives and steals our joy. But God wants us to have ecstasy forever. And you can always be happy, if you fully yield your life to Christ and take care to combat anything that would distract you from Him.

When John saw the new heaven that God would make for His children, he heard a loud voice saying:

> God shall wipe away every tear from their eyes; there shall be no more death, nor sorrow, nor crying; and there shall be no more pain, for the former things have passed away (Rev. 21:4).

The things that steal your joy now will be gone forever when you reach heaven. Then everyone will know that ecstasy is God's gift *forever* to the people that He loves. But you can also know that here and now.

As we have seen, anyone can have ecstasy by receiving the Lord Jesus Christ as the Master of his life. Joy comes whenever a person receives Christ, and it lasts as long as he keeps his thoughts and affections focused on Christ. The mighty overflowing of joy that one has at the moment of conversion can remain with him throughout this life, and through all eternity in heaven.

A Permanent Asset

Ecstasy is not like a fine suit of clothes, which we enjoy as long as the creases are crisp and the colors are fresh, but then throw away. It is not like a delicious meal, which we savor and relish for an hour but forget when we get hungry again. Ecstasy is something we have when we get up and when we go to bed. It is good all the time.

I know this sounds strange to many people, but I've found that it's true: *You can be happy every day of your life.* Your exterior situation does not have to dictate your interior attitude, unless you let it. What shows whether or not you are a happy person is not what happens to you, but how you react to what happens.

Similar problems descend upon different people; some let the problems get them down, while others are able to rise above the problems and grow stronger because of them. It all depends on what's inside. A person who has Christ reigning in his heart can have joy permanently. A person who lets his spirit guide his soul can find a ray of sunshine in every crisis.

Ways to Protect Ecstasy

Earlier we discussed how to nourish the gift of ecstasy. As we close our study of ecstasy, let's consider how to protect it.

Ecstasy: Finding Joy in Living

● *Keep in touch with the Source of ecstasy.* Many Christians think that surrendering to Christ is a once-and-for-all experience. They kneel at an altar and repent of their sins, then go out to keep on living like they did before. No wonder they lose their ecstasy! They have lost touch with Christ, who gives ecstasy.

I lived in England for two years during World War II. There I met a very unhappy man who was the leader of a dance band. Even though his music was much in demand, he seemed disappointed with life.

"You know, I do not understand," he told me one evening. "I attended a church that taught all the basic doctrines of the Christian faith. They told me that if I accepted Christ I would be eternally saved, and I said to myself, 'Well, that's certainly good news!' So I went back to my band. I kept on playing in the night clubs and saloons, and people from the church said I could not do that. I said, 'But I'm saved.' And they said, 'You do not act like you are saved.' But I figure, so what? I may lose some of my reward, but I'm still going to heaven."

"Then why are you so sad?" I asked.

"I don't know," he said. "I'm a Christian—at least they told me I was."

"But you are back playing for the devil," I said.

"Yes," he admitted, "I am going to lose part of my reward for doing this."

We talked for quite awhile and I sensed that he had a deep despair. I asked him if he ever felt happy with life.

"No," he said, lighting another cigarette. "In fact, I wish I was dead."

This man had lost contact with the Source of ecstasy. He was like a limb cut from a tree; without the constant nourishment of Christ, he was dying.

How a person begins and ends his day in large part determines his daily relationship with Jesus.

When I first arrived in England, I was invited to speak at a Christian conference. Another man on the program was Smith Wigglesworth. In the United States I had often heard of Mr. Wigglesworth and his daring faith, so I wanted to become better acquainted with him. He invited me to visit his home in Bradford.

Mr. Wigglesworth was a very gentle person, easy to talk with. Although he was in his eighties and I was in my mid-twenties, we had a great deal in common because we served the same Lord. We became close friends.

After visiting him several times, I said, "Mr. Wigglesworth, you are in your eighties, but you don't act over forty. How is it that every time I come, whether it is raining or the sun is shining brightly, you meet me with such a radiant, joyful expression? How do you do it? Don't you ever feel sad?"

He put his arm around me and drew me close to whisper, "Young man, I don't ask Smith Wigglesworth how he feels."

I drew back, puzzled. "I don't understand," I continued. "Surely there are some mornings when you get up feeling 'under the weather.'"

He shook his head no.

"Then how do you get up?"

"That's simple," he replied. "I lift my feet off the bed, and then I dance all over the bedroom with my hands lifted to Jesus, saying, 'I love You, Lord! I love You because You saved me. I love You because of good health. I love You because of Your goodness and mercy. I love You because You an-

151

swer my prayers. I just love You!' I do that for about ten minutes, giving my love to Jesus and dancing before Him like David.

"Then I take a shower, dress, go downstairs, and answer the mail," he went on. "I read my Bible and pray, especially praying for people who've requested prayer. It's a wonderful life!

"Your problem is that you get up some mornings and say, 'I do not feel good. I have a pain,' and so on. I never do that. I tell myself how I *ought* to feel. I get up and say, 'Smith Wigglesworth, you're feeling fine!' And that sets my course for the day."

This man had learned how to let his spirit talk to his soul, to let his born-again nature talk to his carnal nature. It's as if the spiritual man were saying to the natural man, "Good morning! Get up and get going. You feel good today!" His spirit told his soul what to do, not vice versa; and that kept him in touch with the Source of ecstasy.

Every time I visited him over the next two years, his face was radiant and joyful. He would lock me in his arms and say, "Praise God! I'm so glad to see you!"

Anyone can have this constant, beautiful ecstasy. Stay in touch with the Source of ecstasy, and you will have it.

• *Exert your anointing.* Everyone is God-anointed to do certain things especially well, and the joyful person has God's anointing for joy. If you do not use a gift the Holy Spirit has given you, you will lose it. This certainly applies to ecstasy. If you tell others about it and encourage them to receive it, you will keep it fresh in your own life. But if you try to keep ecstasy to yourself, if you refuse to tell others about it, you will find it withering away.

I believe the Lord is saying, "Use the joy I have

given you. Don't become negative, thinking about world conditions. The world is right on schedule for what I intend to do. Don't worry about the price of gasoline. You may not need to buy as much anyway. And don't complain about the condition of your church; my Son is still the Head of the church, as He's always been. Just sing praises! Let people know you are happy!"

If you become a negative person, you will lose the positive blessing of ecstasy. You cannot keep that positive gift with a negative, skeptical attitude in your heart. So you need to exercise what God has given you.

• *Keep yourself holy.* If you wish to retain your joy forever, retain your spirituality. This pertains to the way you live and act toward others. Paul says, "Denying ungodliness and worldly lusts, we should live soberly, righteously, and godly in the present age" (Tit. 2:12).

Living a godly life does not necessarily make you a social outcast. In fact, other people will often respect you more for being true to the Lord, and your behavior can open the door for sharing Christ with them. A pair of staff members from the Navigators, a nondenominational Christian organization, took a survey of college-age men on a variety of questions about women. At one point in the survey, the interviewers asked what these men appreciated about Christian women. Here are the results:

> They were found to like women who didn't strive for attention and who found their security in God. They appreciated women who did not flirt, who were modest in their dress, and who were sensitive to the feelings of men. They respected a woman of worth, a woman whose beauty was in her character.[2]

This is true in other areas of conduct as well. Your friends will respect you more—and you will respect yourself more—if you discipline yourself to do what you know is right.

• *Avoid the imitators of ecstasy.* I feel compelled to say it again: Do not waste your life with the hollow imitators of ecstasy. Especially avoid the occult and mysticism, which claim to give you god-like wisdom but actually leave you open to satanic powers. Millions of people read their horoscopes in the daily newspapers and plan their activities according to the stars. This practice was born in pagan Babylonian cults and passed down through witchcraft and fortune-telling.

Astrology and other forms of the occult claim to give what God has already given you—joy, gladness, and peace of mind. But if you play with sinister powers that are not of God, you will be walking away from ecstasy. I hope you realize this.

Through the years of my ministry, God has used me to deliver several people who were demon-possessed. Many times I found that these people fell under demonic influences while they were experimenting with the occult.[3] So I know the insidious danger of these things; they can ruin a person's life.

I have often thought that if people ran their businesses like they ran their lives, everyone would be bankrupt. Merchants run their businesses very carefully, guarding against anything that might weaken their position in the marketplace. But how many people are *that* careful about what they bring into their spiritual lives? We are exposed to all manner of cheap sensationalism under the guise of Christianity; how closely do we examine the goods to make sure they're genuine?

Ecstasy Is Yours Forever

Be vigilant about what you bring into your life. Don't swallow an empty substitute for ecstasy.

Ecstasy Tomorrow

The Book of Revelation is one of my favorite portions of Scripture. It tells me about the future and points me to my eternal destiny with the Lord. At the beginning of this chapter I mentioned a passage from Revelation 21 that promises eternal ecstasy in the New Jerusalem that Christ has gone to prepare for His saints. Let us look back to that text and drink deeply of the precious message it has for us:

> And I heard a loud voice out of heaven saying, "Behold, the tabernacle of God is with men, and He shall dwell with them. . . .And God shall wipe away every tear from their eyes; there shall be no more death, nor sorrow, nor crying; and there shall be no more pain, for the former things have passed away" (Rev. 21:3,4).

Imagine living in a place where there will be no more tears, no more pain, and no more death! Won't that be ecstasy! We only have a foretaste of ecstatic living in this present world, but we will have ecstasy in its fullness when we meet God face to face. If you think I am a happy person now, just wait until you see me dancing down those glorious streets paved with gold!

"Oh," you may say, "that is just pie in the sky."

Thank God it is, and I already have a taste of it!

When the saints of heaven cry, "Holy, holy, holy," I will be right there with them, singing at the top of my voice. The joy I have today is not temporary; it is not an emotional roller coaster. It is mine forever, and it is going to keep getting better and better until I get to heaven—and then it's going to skyrocket! I want you to have this ecstasy, too. It begins with Jesus. It begins with salvation. It begins right now.

Notes

I

1. Joni Eareckson and Joe Musser, *Joni* (Minneapolis: World Wide Publications, 1976), pp. 118,119.
2. Clyde M. Narramore, *This Way to Happiness* (Grand Rapids, Mich.: Zondervan, 1958), p. 37.
3. Eugenia Price, *The Burden Is Light!* (Old Tappan, N.J.: Spire Books, 1966), pp. 120,121.
4. Edith Schaeffer, *L'Abri* (Wheaton, Ill.: Tyndale House, 1969), pp. 69,70.

II

1. Joan Winmill Brown, ed., *Day-by-Day with Billy Graham* (Minneapolis: World Wide Publications, 1976), Aug. 2.
2. James Weldon Johnson, *God's Trombones* (New York: Viking Press, 1927), p. 20.
3. Richard H. Harvey, *70 Years of Miracles* (Beaverlodge, Alberta: Horizon Books, 1977), pp. 25–28.

III

1. Harold Lindsell, *The World, the Flesh, and the Devil* (Washington, D.C.: Canon Press, 1974), p. 18.

Ecstasy: Finding Joy in Living

2. Ney Bailey, *Faith Is Not a Feeling* (San Bernardino, Calif.: *Here's Life Publishers*, 1978), p. 18.

IV

1. Warren W. Wiersbe, *The Best of A. W. Tozer* (Grand Rapids, Mich.: Baker, 1978), p. 98.
2. Charles L. Allen, *God's Psychiatry* (New York: Pyramid, 1974), pp. 27,28.
3. F. B. Meyer, *Meet for the Master's Use* (Chicago: Moody Press, n.d.), p. 92.
4. *The Best of A. W. Tozer*, compiled by Warren W. Wiersbe (Grand Rapids, Mich.: Baker, 1978), p. 197.

V

1. R. Buckminster Fuller, *I Seem to Be a Verb* (New York: Bantam Books, 1970), p. 183A.
2. Marshall McLuhan, *Understanding Media* (New York: New American Library, 1964), pp. 59,60.
3. Theodore Lidz, *The Person* (New York: Basic Books, 1976), p. 584.
4. Hannah Whitall Smith, *The Christian's Secret of a Happy Life* (Old Tappan, N.J.: Revell, 1942), p. 50.
5. G. Roger Schoenhals, ed., *When Trouble Comes* (Winona Lake, Ind.: Light and Life Press, 1978), p. 76.
6. Cyvette Guerra, *The Joy Robbers* (Nashville: Impact Books, 1979), p. 43.
7. V. Raymond Edman, *The Disciplines of Life* (Minneapolis: World Wide Publications, 1948), pp. 12,13.
8. Thomas á Kempis, *Of the Imitation of Christ*, trans. Justin McCann (New York: New American Library, 1957), p. 22.

Notes

9. Brother Lawrence, *The Practice of the Presence of God* (Old Tappan, N.J.: Spire Books, 1972), p. 31.

VI

1. "Peace, Perfect Peace."
2. George W. Crane, *Psychology Applied* (Chicago: Hopkins Syndicate, 1956), p. 73.
3. Floyd V. Ruch, ed., *Psychology and Life*, sixth ed. (Chicago: Scott, Foresman and Co., 1963), pp. 346,347.
4. Francis A. Schaeffer, *The God Who Is There* (Downers Grove, Ill.: InterVarsity Press, 1968), p. 13.
5. Maxwell Malz, *Psycho-Cybernetics* (New York: Essandess Special Editions, 1967), p. 92.
6. Tim LaHaye, *The Spirit-Controlled Temperament* (Wheaton, Ill.: Tyndale, 1966), p. 59.
7. Samuel M. Shoemaker, *With the Holy Spirit and with Fire* (Waco, Tex.: Word, 1960), p. 30.

VII

1. D. Elton Trueblood, *The Predicament of Modern Man* (New York: Harper and Brothers, 1944), pp. 70,71.
2. Charles W. Colson, *Born Again* (Old Tappan, N.J.: Chosen Books, 1976), p. 130.

VIII

1. R. A. Torrey, *The God of the Bible* (New York: George H. Doran Co., 1923), p. 163.
2. Mort Crim, *Like It Is!* (Anderson, Ind.: Warner Press, 1970), p. 31.
3. J. Wallace Hamilton, *Ride the Wild Horses!* (Old Tappan, N.J.: Revell, 1952), p. 40.

Ecstasy: Finding Joy in Living

4. Gipsy Smith, *Real Religion* (New York: George H. Doran Co., 1922), p. 18.

5. Ralph Woodworth, *Light in a Dark Place: The Story of Chicago's Oldest Rescue Mission* (Winona Lake, Ind.: Light and Life Press, 1978), p. 31.

6. Jo Petty, ed., *Apples of Gold* (Norwalk, Conn.: C. R. Gibson Co., 1962), p. 62.

7. Merlin R. Carouthers, *Prison to Praise* (Watchung, N.J.: Charisma Books, 1970), p. 37.

IX

1. James F. White, *New Forms of Worship* (Nashville: Abingdon, 1971), p. 52.

X

1. "Fight the Good Fight."

2. Harvey J.S. Blaney, "The First Epistle of John," *Beacon Bible Commentary*, Vol. 10, A. F. Harper, ed. (Kansas City, Mo.: Beacon Hill Press, 1967), p. 370.

3. Donald G. Miller, "The First Letter of John," *The Oxford Annotated Bible*, Herbert G. May and Bruce M. Metzger, eds. (New York: Oxford University Press, 1965), p. 1483.

4. Gloria Gaither, *Make Warm Noises* (Nashville: Impact Books, 1971), p. 41.

5. Joyce Landorf, *The High Cost of Growing* (Nashville: Thomas Nelson, 1978), p. 92.

6. Baker James Cauthren, *Beyond Call* (Nashville: Broadman, 1973), p. 105.

7. Larry Poland, *Spirit Power* (San Bernardino Calif.: Campus Crusade for Christ, 1978), pp. 97,98

XI

1. "In the Cross of Christ I Glory."
2. Carole Mayhall, *Lord, Teach Me Wisdom* (Colorado Springs: Navpress, 1979), p. 132.
3. For a description of some of these experiences, see Lester Sumrall, *Demons: The Answer Book* (Nashville: Thomas Nelson, 1979).